PERPETUAL WAR for PERPETUAL PEACE

ALSO BY GORE VIDAL

GORE VIDAL

PERPETUAL WAR for PERPETUAL PEACE

How We Got to Be So Hated

Thunder's Mouth Press / Nation Books
New York

PERPETUAL WAR FOR PERPETUAL PEACE:
How We Got to Be So Hated

Copyright © 2002 by Gore Vidal

Published by
Thunder's Mouth Press/Nation Books
245 West 17th Street, 11th Floor
New York, NY 10011-5300

Nation Books is a co-publishing venture of the Nation Institute
and Avalon Publishing Group Incorporated.

*The New Theocrats, A Letter to be Delivered, Shredding of the Bill of
Rights,* from *The Last Empire* by Gore Vidal, copyright (c) 2001 by
Gore Vidal. Used by permission of Doubleday, a division of
Random House.

United States Military Operations (pp. 22–41) reprinted by
permission of the Federation of American Scientists.

Library of Congress Cataloging-in-Publication Data
is available for this title.

ISBN 1-56025-405-X

18   17   16   15   14   13   12   11

Book design by Sue Canavan
Printed in the United States of America
Distributed by Publishers Group West

CONTENTS

INTRODUCTION

Gore Vidal

It is a law of physics (still on the books when last I looked) that in nature there is no action without reaction. The same appears to be true in human nature—that is, history. In the last six years, two dates are apt to be remembered for longer than usual in the United States of Amnesia: April 19, 1995, when a much-decorated infantry soldier called Timothy McVeigh blew up a federal building in Oklahoma City, killing 168 innocent men, women, and children. Why? McVeigh told us at eloquent length, but our rulers and their media preferred to depict him as a sadistic, crazed monster—not a good person like the rest of us—who had done it just for kicks. On September 11, 2001, Osama bin Laden and his Islamic terrorist organization struck at Manhattan and the Pentagon. The Pentagon Junta in charge of our affairs programmed their president to tell us that bin Laden was an "evildoer" who envied us our goodness and wealth and freedom.

None of these explanations made much sense, but our rulers for more than half a century have made sure that we are never to be told the truth about anything that our government has done to other people, not to mention, in McVeigh's case, our own. All we are left with are blurred covers of *Time* and *Newsweek* where monstrous figures from Hieronymus Bosch stare out at us, hellfire in their eyes, while the *New York Times* and its chorus of imitators spin complicated stories about mad Osama and cowardly McVeigh, thus convincing most Americans that only a couple of freaks would ever dare strike at a nation that sees itself as close to perfection as any human society can come. That our ruling junta might have seriously provoked McVeigh (a heartland American hero of the Gulf War) and Osama, a would-be Muslim Defender of the Faith, was never dealt with.

Things just happen out there in the American media, and we consumers don't need to be told the why of anything. Certainly those of us who are in the why-business have a difficult time getting through the corporate-sponsored American media, as I discovered when I tried to explain

McVeigh in *Vanity Fair,* or when, since September 11, my attempts to get published have met with failure.

Another silenced September voice was that of Arno J. Mayer, professor emeritus of history at Princeton, whose piece entitled "Untimely Reflections" was turned down everywhere in the United States, including by *The Nation,* where I have been a contributing editor for many years (and where *my* untimely reflections on September 11 were also turned down). Mayer published his piece in the French newspaper *Le Monde.* He wrote, in part:

> Until now, in modern times, acts of individual
> terror have been the weapon of the weak and
> the poor, while acts of state and economic terror
> have been the weapons of the strong. In both
> types of terror it is, of course, important to dis-
> tinguish between target and victim. This distinc-
> tion is crystal clear in the fatal hit on the World
> Trade Center: the target is a prominent symbol
> and hub of globalizing corporate financial and
> economic power; the victim the hapless and
> partly subaltern workforce. Such distinction
> does not apply to the strike on the Pentagon: it
> houses the supreme military command—the
> *ultima ratio regnum*—of capitalist globalization

even if it entails, in the Pentagon's own language, "collateral" damage to human life.

In any case, since 1947 America has been the chief and pioneering perpetrator of "preemptive" state terror, exclusively in the Third World and therefore widely dissembled. Besides the unexceptional subversion and overthrow of governments in competition with the Soviet Union during the Cold War, Washington has resorted to political assassinations, surrogate death squads, and unseemly freedom fighters (e.g., bin Laden). It masterminded the killing of Lumumba and Allende; and it unsuccessfully tried to put to death Castro, Khadafi, and Saddam Hussein; and vetoed all efforts to rein in not only Israel's violation of international agreements and U.S. resolutions but also its practice of preemptive state terror.

I should point out that *Le Monde* is a moderately conservative highbrow publication and, for decades, a supporter of Israel. Arno Mayer himself spent "school days" in a German concentration camp.

My own September 11 piece was subsequently published in Italian, in a book like this one. To everyone's astonishment it was an instant best-seller, and then translated in a dozen other languages. With both bin Laden and McVeigh, I thought it useful to describe the various provocations on our side that drove them to such terrible acts.

September 11, 2001
(A Tuesday)

SEPTEMBER 11, 2001
(A TUESDAY)

According to the Koran, it was on a Tuesday that Allah created darkness. Last September 11 when suicide pilots were crashing commercial airliners into crowded American buildings, I did not have to look to the calendar to see what day it was: Dark Tuesday was casting its long shadow across Manhattan and along the Potomac River. I was also not surprised that despite the seven or so trillion dollars that we have spent since 1950 on what is euphemistically called "Defense," there would have been no advance warning from the FBI or CIA or Defense Intelligence Agency.

While the Bushites have been eagerly preparing for the last war but two—missiles from North Korea, clearly marked with flags, would rain down on Portland, Oregon, only to be intercepted by our missile-shield balloons—the foxy Osama bin Laden knew that all *he* needed for his holy war on the infidel were fliers willing to kill themselves along with those random passengers who happened to be aboard hijacked airliners.

The telephone keeps ringing. In summer I live south of Naples, Italy. Italian newspapers, TV, radio want comment. So do I. I have written lately about Pearl Harbor. Now I get the same question over and over: Isn't this exactly like Sunday morning, December 7, 1941? No, it's not, I say. As far as we *now* know, we had no warning of Tuesday's attack. Of course, our government has many, many secrets that our enemies always seem to know about in advance but our people are not told of until years later, if at all. President Roosevelt provoked the Japanese to attack us at Pearl Harbor. I describe the various steps he took in a book, *The Golden Age*. We now know what was on his mind: coming to England's aid against Japan's ally, Hitler, a virtuous plot that ended triumphantly for the human race. But what was—is—on bin Laden's mind?

For several decades there has been an unrelenting demonization of the Muslim world in the American media. Since I am a loyal American, I am not supposed to tell you *why* this has taken place, but then it is not usual for us to examine why *anything* happens; we simply accuse others of motiveless malignity. "We are good," G.W. proclaims, "They are evil," which wraps that one up in a neat package.

Later, Bush himself put, as it were, the bow on the package in an address to a joint session of Congress where he shared with them—as well as with the rest of us somewhere over the Beltway—his profound knowledge of Islam's wiles and ways: "They hate what they see right here in this Chamber." I suspect a million Americans nodded sadly in front of their TV sets. "*Their* leaders are self-appointed. They hate our freedoms, our freedom of religion, our freedom of speech, our freedom to vote and assemble and disagree with each other." At this plangent moment what American's gorge did not rise like a Florida chad to the bait?

Should the forty-four-year-old Saudi Arabian, bin Laden, prove to be the prime mover, we still know surprisingly little about him. The six-foot seven-inch Osama enters history in 1979 as a guerrilla warrior working alongside the CIA to defend Afghanistan against the invading Soviets. Was he anticommunist? Irrelevant question. He wants no infidels of any sort in the Islamic world. Described as fabulously wealthy, Osama is worth "only" a few million dollars, according to a relative. It was his father who created a fabulous fortune with a construction company that specialized in building palaces for the Saudi royal family. That company is now worth several billion dollars, presumably shared by Osama's fifty-four brothers and sisters. Although he speaks perfect English, he was educated entirely at

Jiddah. He has never traveled outside the Arabian Peninsula. Several siblings lived in the Boston area and have given large sums to Harvard. We are told that much of his family appears to have disowned him and many of his assets in the Saudi kingdom have been frozen.

Where does Osama's money now come from? He is a superb fund-raiser for Allah but only within the Arab world; contrary to legend, he has taken no CIA money. He warned the Saudi king that Saddam Hussein was going to invade Kuwait. Osama assumed that after his own victories as a guerrilla against the Russians, he and his organization would be used by the Saudis to stop the Iraqis. To Osama's horror, King Fahd sent for the Americans: thus were infidels established on the sacred soil of Mohammed. "This was," he said, "the most shocking moment of my life." "Infidel," in his sense, does not mean anything of great moral consequence—like cheating sexually on your partner; rather it means lack of faith in Allah—the one God—and in his prophet Mohammed.

Osama persuaded four thousand Saudis to go to Afghanistan for military training by his group. In 1991, Osama moved on to Sudan. In 1994, when the Saudis withdrew his citizenship, Osama was already a legendary figure in the Islamic world and so, like Shakespeare's Coriolanus, he could tell the royal Saudis, "I banish you. There is a world elsewhere." Unfortunately, that world is us.

In a twelve-page "declaration of war," Osama presented himself as the potential liberator of the Muslim world from the great Satan of modern corruption, the United States.

Osama's organization blew up two of our embassies in Africa, and put a hole in the side of an American warship off Yemen, Clinton lobbed a missile at a Sudanese aspirin factory, and so on to the events of Black Tuesday. G. W. Bush was then transformed before our eyes into the cheerleader that he had been in prep school. First he promised us not only "a new war" but a "secret war" and, best of all, according to the twinkle in his eye, "a very long war." Meanwhile, "this administration will not talk about any plans we may or may not have . . . We're going to find these evildoers and we're going to hold them accountable," along with the other devils who have given Osama shelter.

As of the first month of 2002, the Pentagon Junta pretends that the devastation of Afghanistan by our high-flying air force has been a great victory (no one mentions that the Afghans were not an American enemy—it was like destroying Palermo in order to eliminate the Mafia). In any case, we may never know what, if anything, was won or lost (other than much of the Bill of Rights).

A member of the Pentagon Junta, Rumsfeld, a skilled stand-up comic, daily made fun of a large group of "journalists" on prime-time TV. At great, and often amusing, length,

Rummy tells us nothing about our losses and their losses. He did seem to believe that the sentimental Osama was holed up in a cave on the Pakistan border instead of settled in a palace in Indonesia or Malaysia, two densely populated countries where he is admired and we are not. In any case, never before in our long history of undeclared unconstitutional wars have we, the American people, been treated with such impish disdain—so many irrelevant spear carriers to be highly taxed (those of us who are not rich) and occasionally invited to participate in the odd rigged poll.

When Osama was four years old I arrived in Cairo for a conversation with Nasser, to appear in *Look* magazine. I was received by Mohammed Hekal, Nasser's chief adviser. Nasser himself was not to be seen. He was at the Barricade, his retreat on the Nile; he had just survived an assassination attempt. Hekal spoke perfect English; he was sardonic, worldly. "We are studying the Koran for hints on birth control." A sigh.

"Not helpful?"

"Not very. But we keep looking for a text." We talked off and on for a week. Nasser wanted to modernize Egypt. But there was a reactionary, religious element . . . Another sigh. Then a surprise. "We've found something very odd, the young village boys—the bright ones that we are educating to be engineers, chemists and so on, are turning religious on us."

"Right wing?"

"Very." Hekal was a spiritual son of our eighteenth-century enlightenment. I thought of Hekal on Dark Tuesday when one of his modernized Arab generation had, in the name of Islam, struck at what had been, forty years earlier, Nasser's model for a modern state. Yet Osama seemed, from all accounts, no more than a practicing, as opposed to zealous, Muslim. Ironically, he was trained as an engineer. Understandably, he dislikes the United States as symbol and as fact. But when our clients, the Saudi royal family, allowed American troops to occupy the Prophet's holy land, Osama named the fundamental enemy "the Crusader Zionist Alliance." Thus, in a phrase, he defined himself and reminded his critics that he is a Wahabi Muslim, a Puritan activist not unlike our Falwell/Robertson zanies, only serious. He would go to war against the United States, "the head of the serpent." Even more ambitiously, he would rid all the Muslim states of their western-supported regimes, starting with that of his native land. The word "Crusader" was the giveaway. In the eyes of many Muslims, the Christian west, currently in alliance with Zionism, has for a thousand years tried to dominate the lands of the Umma—the true believers. That is why Osama is seen by so many simple folk as the true heir to Saladin, the great warrior king who defeated Richard of England and the western crusaders.

Who was Saladin? Dates 1138–1193. He was an
Armenian Kurd. In the century before his birth, western
Christians had established a kingdom at Jerusalem, to the
horror of the Islamic Faithful. Much as the United States
used the Gulf War as pretext for our current occupation of
Saudi Arabia, Saladin raised armies to drive out the Crusaders.
He conquered Egypt, annexed Syria, and finally smashed
the Kingdom of Jerusalem in a religious war that pitted
Mohammedan against Christian. He united and "purified"
the Muslim world and though Richard Lion-heart was the
better general, in the end he gave up and went home. As
one historian put it, Saladin "typified the Mohammedan
utter self-surrender to a sacred cause." But he left no government behind him, no political system because, as he
himself said, "My troops will do nothing save when I ride
at their head . . . " Now his spirit has returned with a
vengeance.

The Bush administration, though eerily inept in all but its
principal task, which is to exempt the rich from taxes, has
casually torn up most of the treaties to which civilized
nations subscribe—like the Kyoto Accords or the nuclear
missile agreement with Russia. The Bushites go about their

relentless plundering of the Treasury and now, thanks to Osama, Social Security (a supposedly untouchable trust fund), which, like Lucky Strike green, has gone to a war currently costing us $3 billion a month. They have also allowed the FBI and CIA either to run amok or not budge at all, leaving us, the very first "indispensable" and—at popular request—last global empire, rather like the Wizard of Oz doing his odd pretend-magic tricks while hoping not to be found out. Meanwhile, G.W. booms, "Either you are with us or you are with the Terrorists." That's known as asking for it.

To be fair, one cannot entirely blame the current Oval One for our incoherence. Though his predecessors have generally had rather higher IQs than his, they, too, assiduously served the 1 percent that owns the country while allowing everyone else to drift. Particularly culpable was Bill Clinton. Although the most able chief executive since FDR, Clinton, in his frantic pursuit of election victories, set in place the trigger for a police state that his successor is now happily squeezing.

Police state? What's that all about? In April 1996, one year after the Oklahoma City bombing, President Clinton signed into law the Anti-Terrorism and Effective Death Penalty Act, a so-called conference bill in which many grubby hands played a part, including the bill's cosponsor, Senate Majority leader Dole. Although Clinton, in order to win elections, did many unwise and opportunistic things, he seldom, like Charles II, ever said an unwise one. But faced with opposition to antiterrorism legislation that not only gives the attorney general the power to use the armed services against the civilian population, neatly nullifying the Posse Comitatus Act of 1878, it also, selectively, suspends habeas corpus, the heart of Anglo-American liberty. Clinton attacked his critics as "unpatriotic." Then, wrapped in the flag, he spoke from the throne: "There is nothing patriotic about our pretending that you can love your country but despise your government." This is breathtaking since it includes, at one time or another, most of us. Put another way, was a German in 1939 who said that he detested the Nazi dictatorship unpatriotic?

There have been ominous signs that our fragile liberties have been dramatically at risk since the 1970s when the white-shirt-blue-suit-discreet-tie FBI reinvented itself from a corps of "generalists," trained in law and accounting, into a confrontational "Special Weapons and Tactics" (aka SWAT) Green Beret–style army of warriors who like to dress up in camouflage or black ninja clothing and, depending on the caper, ski masks. In the early '80s an FBI super-SWAT team, the *Hostage 270 Rescue Team*, was formed. As so often happens in United States–speak, this group specialized not in freeing hostages or saving lives but in murderous attacks on groups that offended them like the Branch Davidians—evangelical Christians who were living peaceably in their own compound at Waco, Texas, until an FBI SWAT team, illegally using army tanks, killed eighty-two of them, including twenty-five children. This was 1993.

Post Tuesday, SWAT teams can now be used to go after suspect Arab Americans or, indeed, anyone who might be guilty of terrorism, a word without legal definition (how can you fight terrorism by suspending habeas corpus since those who want their corpuses released from prison are already locked up?). But in the post–Oklahoma City trauma, Clinton said that those who did not support his draconian legislation were terrorist coconspirators who wanted to turn "America into a safe house for terrorists." If the cool Clinton could so froth, what are we to expect from the overheated post-Tuesday Bush?

Incidentally, those who were shocked by Bush the Younger's shout that we are now "at war" with Osama should have quickly put on their collective thinking caps. Since a nation can only be at war with another nation–state, why did our smoldering if not yet burning bush come up with such a war cry? Think hard. This will count against your final grade. Give up? Well, most insurance companies have a rider that they need not pay for damage done by "an act of war." Although the men and women around Bush know nothing of war and less of our Constitution, they understand fund-raising. For this wartime exclusion, Hartford Life would soon be breaking open its piggy bank to finance Republicans for years to come. But the mean-spirited *Washington Post* pointed out that under U.S. case law, *only* a sovereign nation, not a bunch of radicals, can commit an "act of war." Good try, G.W. This now means that we the people, with our tax money, will be allowed to bail out the insurance companies, a rare privilege not afforded to just any old generation.

Although the American people have no direct means of influencing their government, their "opinions" are occasionally sampled through polls. According to a November 1995 CNN-*Time* poll, 55 percent of the people believe "the federal government has become so powerful that it poses a threat to the rights of ordinary citizens." Three days after Dark Tuesday, 74 percent said they thought, "It would be necessary for Americans to give up some of their personal freedoms." Eighty-six percent favored guards and metal detectors at public buildings and events. Thus, as the police state settles comfortably in place, one can imagine Cheney and Rumsfeld studying these figures, transfixed with joy. "It's what they always wanted, Dick."

"And to think we never knew, Don."

"Thanks to those liberals, Dick."

"We'll get those bastards now, Don."

It seems forgotten by our amnesiac media that we once energetically supported Saddam Hussein in Iraq's war against Iran and so Saddam thought, not unnaturally, that we wouldn't mind his taking over Kuwait's filling stations. Overnight our employee became Satan—and so remains, as we torment his people in the hope that they will rise up and overthrow him—as the Cubans were supposed, in their U.S.-imposed poverty, to have dismissed Castro for his ongoing refusal to allow the Kennedy brothers to murder him in their so-called Operation Mongoose. Our imperial disdain for the lesser breeds did not go unnoticed by the latest educated generation of Saudi Arabians, and by their evolving leader, Osama bin Laden, whose moment came in 2001 when a weak American president took office in questionable circumstances.

The New York Times is the principal dispenser of opinion received from corporate America. It generally stands tall, or tries to. Even so, as of September 13 the *NYT*'s editorial columns were all slightly off-key.

Under the heading "Demands of Leadership" the *NYT* was upbeat, sort of. It's going to be okay if you work hard and keep your eye on the ball, Mr. President. Apparently Bush is "facing multiple challenges, but his most important job is a simple matter of leadership." Thank God. Not only is that *all* it takes, but it's *simple*, too! For a moment . . . The *NYT* then slips into the way things look as opposed to the way they ought to look. "The Administration spent much of yesterday trying to overcome the impression that Mr. Bush showed weakness when he did not return to Washington after the terrorists struck." But from what I could tell no one cared, while some of us felt marginally safer, that the national silly-billy was trapped in his Nebraska bunker. Patiently, the *NYT* spells it out for Bush and for us, too. "In the days ahead, Mr. Bush may be asking the nation to support military actions that many citizens, particularly those with relations in the service, will find alarming. He must show that he knows what he is doing." Well, that's a bull's-eye. If only FDR had got letters like that from Arthur Krock at the old *NYT*.

Finally, Anthony Lewis thinks it wise to eschew Bushite unilateralism in favor of cooperation with other nations in order to contain Tuesday's darkness by *understanding its origin* (my emphasis) while ceasing our provocations of cultures opposed to us and our arrangements. Lewis, unusually for a *New York Times* writer, favors peace now. So do I. But then we are old and have been to the wars and value our fast-diminishing freedoms unlike those jingoes now beating their tom-toms in Times Square in favor of all-out war for other Americans to fight.

As usual, the political columnist who has made the most sense of all this is William Pfaff in the international *Herald Tribune* (September 17, 2001). Unlike the provincial war lovers at the *New York Times*, he is appalled by the spectacle of an American president who declined to serve his country in Vietnam, howling for war against not a nation or even a religion but one man and his accomplices, a category that will ever widen.

> Pfaff: The riposte of a civilized nation: one that believes in good, in human society and does oppose evil, has to be narrowly focused and, above all, intelligent.
>
> Missiles are blunt weapons. Those terrorists are smart enough to make others bear the price for what they have done, and to exploit the results.
>
> A maddened U.S. response that hurts still others is what they want: It will fuel the hatred that already fires the self-righteousness about their criminal acts against the innocent.
>
> What the United States needs is cold reconsideration of how it has arrived at this pass. It needs, even more, to foresee disasters that might lie in the future.

• • •

War is the no-win all-lose option. The time has come to put the good Kofi Annan to use. As glorious as total revenge will be for our war lovers, a truce between Saladin and the Crusader-Zionists is in the interest of the entire human race. Long before the dread monotheists got their hands on history's neck, we had been taught how to handle feuds by none other than the god Apollo as dramatized by Aeschylus in *Eumenides* (a polite Greek term for the Furies who keep us daily company on CNN). Orestes, for the sin of matricide, cannot rid himself of the Furies who hound him wherever he goes. He appeals to the god Apollo who tells him to go to the UN—also known as the citizens' assembly at Athens— which he does and is acquitted on the ground that blood feuds must be ended or they will smolder forever, generation after generation, and great towers shall turn to flame and incinerate us all until "the thirsty dust shall never more suck up the darkly steaming blood . . . and vengeance crying death for death! But man with man and state with state shall vow the pledge of common hate and common friendship, that for man has oft made blessing out of ban, be ours until all time." Let Annan mediate between East and West before there is nothing left of either of us to salvage.

The awesome physical damage Osama and company did to us on Dark Tuesday is as nothing compared to the knockout blow to our vanishing liberties—the Anti-Terrorism Act of 1996 combined with the recent requests to Congress for additional special powers to wiretap without judicial order; to deport lawful permanent residents, visitors, and undocumented immigrants without due process; and so on. As I write, U.S. "Concentration Camp X-Ray" is filling up at marine base Quantanamo Bay, Cuba. No one knows whether or not these unhappy residents are prisoners of war or just plain evildoers. In any case, they were kidnapped in Afghanistan by U.S. forces and now appear to be subject to kangaroo courts when let out of their cages.

This is from a pre-Osama text: "Restrictions on personal liberty, on the right of free expression of opinion, including freedom of the press; on the rights of assembly and associations; and violations of the privacy of postal, telegraphic, and telephonic communications and warrants for house searches, orders for confiscations as well as restrictions on property, are also permissible beyond the legal limits otherwise prescribed." The tone is familiar. Clinton? Bush? Ashcroft? No. It is from Hitler's 1933 speech calling for "an Enabling Act" for "the protection of the People and the State" after the catastrophic Reichstag fire that the Nazis had secretly lit.

Only one congresswoman, Barbara Lee of California, voted against the additional powers granted the president.

Meanwhile, a *New York Times*–CBS poll noted that only 6 percent now opposed military action while a substantial majority favored war "even if many thousands of innocent civilians are killed." Simultaneously, Bush's approval rating has soared, but then, traditionally, in war, the president is totemic like the flag. When Kennedy got his highest rating after the debacle of the Bay of Pigs, he observed, characteristically, "It would seem that the worse you fuck up in this job the more popular you get." Bush, father and son, may yet make it to Mount Rushmore though it might be cheaper to redo Barbara Bush's look-alike, George Washington, by adding two strings of Teclas to his limestone neck—in memoriam, as it were.

Finally, the physical damage Osama and friends can do us—terrible as it has been thus far—is as nothing as to what he is doing to our liberties. Once alienated, an "unalienable right" is apt to be forever lost, in which case we are no longer even remotely the last best hope of earth but merely a seedy imperial state whose citizens are kept in line by SWAT teams and whose way of death, not life, is universally imitated.

Since V-J Day 1945 ("Victory over Japan" and the end of World War II), we have been engaged in what the historian Charles A. Beard called "perpetual war for perpetual peace." I have occasionally referred to our "enemy of the month club": each month we are confronted by a new horrendous enemy at whom we must strike before he destroys us. I have been accused of exaggeration, so here's the scoreboard from Kosovo (1999) back to Berlin Airlift (1948–49). You will note that the compilers, Federation of American Scientists, record a number of our wars as "ongoing," even though many of us have forgotten about them. We are given, under "Name," many fanciful Defense Department titles like *Urgent Fury*, which was Reagan's attack on the island of Grenada, a month-long caper that General Haig disloyally said could have been handled more efficiently by the Provincetown police department. (Question marks are from compilers.)

CURRENT OPERATIONS

Name	Locale
Joint Guardian	Kosovo
Allied Force/Noble Anvil	Kosovo
Determined Force	Kosovo
Cobalt Flash	Kosovo
Shining Hope	Kosovo
Sustain Hope/Allied Harbour	Kosovo
Provide Refuge	Kosovo
Open Arms	Kosovo
Eagle Eye	Kosovo
Determined Falcon	Kosovo & Albania
Determined Effort	Bosnia-Herzegovina
Joint Endeavor	Bosnia-Herzegovina
Joint Guard	Bosnia-Herzegovina
Joint Forge	Bosnia-Herzegovina
DELIBERATE FORCE	Bosnian Serbs
Quick Lift	Croatia
Nomad Vigil	Albania
Nomad Endeavor	Taszar, Hungary
Able Sentry	Serbia-Macedonia
Deny Flight	Bosnia-Herzegovina
Decisive Endeavor/Decisive Edge	Bosnia-Herzegovina
Decisive Guard/Deliberate Guard	Bosnia-Herzegovina
Deliberate Forge	Bosnia-Herzegovina

Dates	U.S. Forces Involved
11 Jun 1999–TDB 200?	
23 Mar 1999–10 Jun 1999	
08 Oct 1998–23 Mar 1999	
05 Apr 1999–Fall 1999	
16 Oct 1998–24 Mar 1999	
15 Jun 1998–16 Jun 1998	
Jul 1995–Dec 1995	
Dec 1995–Dec 1996	
Dec 1996–20 Jun 1998	
20 June 1998–Present	6,900
29 Aug 1995–21 Sep 1995	
03 Jul 1995–11 Aug 1995	
01 Jul 1995–05 Nov 1996	
Mar 1996–Present	
05 Jul 1994–Present	
12 Apr 1993–20 Dec 1995	2,000
Jan 1996–Dec 1996	??
Dec 1996–20 Jun 1998	??
20 Jun 1998–Present	

CURRENT OPERATIONS

Name	Locale
Sky Monitor	Bosnia-Herzegovina
Maritime Monitor	Adriatic Sea
Maritime Guard	Adriatic Sea
Sharp Guard	Adriatic Sea
Decisive Enhancement	Adriatic Sea
Determined Guard	Adriatic Sea
Provide Promise	Bosnia

SOUTHWEST ASIA

Name	Locale
[none] (air strike)	Iraq
[none] (cruise missile strike)	Iraq
[none] (cruise missile strike)	Iraq
DESERT STRIKE	Iraq
DESERT THUNDER	Iraq
DESERT FOX	Iraq
Shining Presence	Israel
Phoenix Scorpion IV	Iraq
Phoenix Scorpion III	Iraq
Phoenix Scorpion II	Iraq
Phoenix Scorpion I	Iraq
Desert Focus	Saudi Arabia
Vigilant Warrior	Kuwait

Dates	U.S. Forces Involved
16 Oct 1992–Present	
16 Jul 1992–22 Nov 1992	??
22 Nov 1992–15 Jun 1993	??
15 Jun 1993–Dec 1995	11,700
Dec 1995–19 Jun 1996	??
Dec 1996–Present	??
03 Jul 1992–Mar 1996	1,000

Dates	U.S. Forces Involved
26 Jun 1993–13 Jan 1993	
13 Jan 1993–17 Jan 1993	
17 Jan 1993–26 Jun 1993	
03 Sep 1996–04 Sep 1996	
Feb 1998–16 Dec 1998	
16 Dec 1998–20 Dec 1998	
Dec 1998–Dec 1998	
Dec 1998–Dec 1998	
Nov 1998–Nov 1998	
Feb 1998–Feb 1998	
Nov 1997–Nov 1997	
Jul 1996–Present	
Oct 1994–Nov 1994	

SOUTHWEST ASIA

Name	Locale
Vigilant Sentinel	Kuwait
Intrinsic Action	Kuwait
Desert Spring	Kuwait
Iris Gold	SW Asia
Pacific Haven/Quick Transit	Iraq > Guam
Provide Comfort	Kurdistan
Provide Comfort II	Kurdistan
Northern Watch	Kurdistan
Southern Watch	Southwest Asia/Iraq
Desert Falcon	Saudi Arabia

OTHER OPERATIONS

Name	Locale
Korea	Korea
New Horizons	Central America
Sierra Leone NEO	Sierra Leone
MONUC [UN PKO]	DR Congo
Resolute Response	Africa
Gatekeeper	California
Hold-the-Line	Texas
Safeguard	Arizona
Golden Pheasant	Honduras
Alliance	U.S. southern border

Dates	U.S. Forces Involved
Aug 1995–15 Feb 1997	
01 Dec 1995–01 Oct 1999	
01 Oct 1999–Present	
?? 1993–Present	
15 Sep 1996–16 Dec 1996	
05 Apr 1991–Dec 1994	42,500
24 Jul 1991–31 Dec 1996	??
31 Dec 1996–Present	1,100
1991–Present	14,000
1991–Present	

Dates	U.S. Forces Involved
Ongoing	
Ongoing	
May 2000	
Feb 2000–Ongoing	
Aug 1998–Present	
1995–Present	
1995–Present	
1995–Present	
Mar 1988–Present	
1986–Present	

OTHER OPERATIONS

Name	Locale
Provide Hope I	Former Soviet Union
Provide Hope II	Former Soviet Union
Provide Hope III	Former Soviet Union
Provide Hope IV	Former Soviet Union
Provide Hope V	Former Soviet Union

COUNTERDRUG OPERATIONS

Name	Locale
Coronet Nighthawk	Central/South America
Coronet Oak	Central/South America
Selva Verde	Colombia
Badge	Kentucky
Ghost Dancer	Oregon
Greensweep	California
Grizzly	California
Wipeout	Hawaii
Ghost Zone	Bolivia
Constant Vigil	Bolivia
Support Justice	South America
Steady State	South America
Green Clover	South America
Laser Strike	South America
Agate Path	CONUS

Dates	U.S. Forces Involved
10 Feb 1992–26 Feb 1992	
15 Apr 1992–29 Jul 1992	
1993?–1993?	
10 Jan 1994–19 Dec 1994	
06 Nov 1998–10 May 1999	

Dates	U.S. Forces Involved
1991–Present	
Oct 1977–17 Feb 1999	
1995–Present	
1990–Present?	
1990–Present?	
Jul 1990–Aug 1990	
1990–Present?	
1990–Present	
Mar 1990–1993?	
199?–??	
1991–1994	
1994–Apr 1996	
199?–199?	
Apr 1996–Present	
1989–???	

COUNTERDRUG OPERATIONS

Name	Locale
Enhanced Ops	CONUS

COMPLETED OPERATIONS

Name	Locale
Silent Promise	Mozambique/South Africa
Fundamental Response	Venezuela
Stabilize	Timor
Avid Response	Turkey
Strong Support [Fuerte Apoyo]	Central America
Infinite Reach	Sudan/Afganistan
Shepherd Venture	Guinea-Bissau
[none]	Asmara, Eritrea NEO
Noble Response	Kenya
Bevel Edge	Cambodia
Noble Obelisk	Sierra Leone
Guardian Retrieval	Congo (formerly Zaire)
Silver Wake	Albania
Guardian Assistance	Zaire/Rwanda/Uganda
Assurance/Phoenix Tusk	Zaire/Rwanda/Uganda
Quick Response	Central African Republic
Assured Response	Liberia
Zorro II	Mexico
Third Taiwan Straits Crisis	Taiwan Strait

Dates	U.S. Forces Involved
???–Present	

Dates	U.S. Forces Involved
Feb 2000–? Apr 2000	
20 Dec 1999–Early 2000	
11 Sep 1999–Nov 1999	
18 Aug 1999–Sep 1999	
Oct 1998–10 Feb 1999	5,700
20 Aug 1998–20 Aug 1998	
10 Jun 1998–17 Jun 1998	130
05 Jun 1998–06 Jun 1998	130
21 Jan 1998–25 Mar 1998	
Jul 1997–Jul 1997	
May 1997–Jun 1997	
Mar 1997–Jun 1997	
14 Mar 1997–26 Mar 1997	
15 Nov 1996–27 Dec 1996	
15 Nov 1996–27 Dec 1996	
May 1996–Aug 1996	
Apr 1996–Aug 1996	
Dec 1995–02 May 1996	
21 Jul 1995–23 Mar 1996	

COMPLETED OPERATIONS

Name	Locale
Safe Border	Peru/Ecuador
United Shield	Somalia
Uphold/Restore Democracy	Haiti
Quiet Resolve/Support Hope	Rwanda
Safe Haven/Safe Passage	Cuba > Panama
Sea Signal/JTF-160	Haiti > Guantanamo, Cub
Distant Runner	Rwanda NEO
Korean Nuclear Crisis	North Korea
[none]	Liberian NEO
Provide Relief	Somalia
Restore Hope	Somalia
Continue Hope	Somalia
Provide Transition	Angola
Garden Plot	Los Angeles, CA
Silver Anvil	Sierra Leone NEO
GTMO	Haiti > Guantanamo, Cub
Safe Harbor	Haiti > Guantanamo, Cub
Quick Lift	Zaire
Victor Squared	Haiti NEO
Fiery Vigil	Philippines NEO
Productive Effort/Sea Angel	Bangledesh
Eastern Exit	Somalia

Dates	U.S. Forces Involved
1995–30 Jun 1999	
03 Jan 1995–25 Mar 1995	4,000
19 Sep 1994–31 Mar 1995	21,000
22 Jul 1994–30 Sep 1994	2,592
06 Sep 1994–01 Mar 1995	
18 May 1994–Feb 1996	
09 Apr 1994–15 Apr 1994	
10 Feb 1993–Jun 1994	
22 Oct 1992–25 Oct 1992	
14 Aug 1992–08 Dec 1992	??
04 Dec 1992–04 May 1993	26,000
04 May 1993–Dec 1993	??
03 Aug 1992–09 Oct 1992	
May 1992	4,500
02 May 1992–05 May 1992	
23 Nov 1991	
1992	
24 Sep 1991–07 Oct 1991	
Sep 1991	
Jun 1991	
May 1991–Jun 1991	
02 Jan 1991–11 Jan 1991	

COMPLETED OPERATIONS

Name	Locale
DESERT STORM	Southwest Asia
Desert Shield	Southwest Asia
Imminent Thunder	Southwest Asia
Proven Force	Southwest Asia
DESERT SWORD/DESERT SABRE	Southwest Asia
Desert Calm	Southwest Asia
Desert Farewell	Southwest Asia
Steel Box/Golden Python	Johnston Island
Sharp Edge	Liberia

COLD WAR ERA

Name	Locale
Classic Resolve	Philippines
Hawkeye	St. Croix, U.S. Virgin Islands
Nimrod Dancer	Panama
JUST CAUSE	Panama
Promote Liberty	Panama
ERNEST WILL	Persian Gulf
PRAYING MANTIS	Persian Gulf
Blast Furnace	Bolivia
EL DORADO CANYON	Libya
Attain Document	Libya
Achille Lauro	Mediterranean

Dates	U.S. Forces Involved
02 Aug 1990–17 Jan 1991	
Nov 1990–Nov 1990	
17 Jan 1991–28 Feb 1991	
24 Feb 1991–28 Feb 1991	555,000
01 Mar 1991–01 Jan 1992	
01 Jan 1992–1992?	
26 Jul 1990–18 Nov 1990	
May 1990–08 Jan 1991	

Dates	U.S. Forces Involved
Nov 1989–Dec 1989	
20 Sep 1989–17 Nov 1989	
May 1989–20 Dec 1989	
20 Dec 1989–31 Jan 1990	
31 Jan 1990–??	
24 Jul 1987–02 Aug 1990	
17 Apr 1988–19 Apr 1988	
Jul 1986–Nov 1986	
12 Apr 1986–17 Apr 1986	
26 Jan 1986–29 Mar 1986	
07 Oct 1985–11 Oct 1985	

COLD WAR ERA

Name	Locale
Intense Look	Red Sea/Gulf of Suez
URGENT FURY	Grenada
Arid Farmer	Chad/Sudan
Early Call	Egypt/Sudan
U.S. Multinational Force [USMNF]	Lebanon
Bright Star	Egypt
Gulf of Sidra	Libya / Mediterranean
RMT (Rocky Mountain Transfer)	Colorado
Central America	El Salvador/Nicaragua
Creek Sentry	Poland
SETCON II	Colorado
EAGLE CLAW/Desert One	Iran
ROK Park Succession Crisis	Korea
Elf One	Saudi Arabia
Yemen	Iran/Yemen/Indian Ocean
Red Bean	Zaire
Ogaden Crisis	Somalia/Ethiopia
SETCON I	Colorado
Paul Bunyan/Tree Incident	Korea
Mayaguez Operation	Cambodia
New Life	Vietnam NEO
Frequent Wind	Evacuation of Saigon
Eagle Pull	Cambodia

Dates	U.S. Forces Involved
Jul 1984–Jul 1984	
23 Oct 1983–21 Nov 1983	
Aug 1983–Aug 1983	
18 Mar 1983–Aug 1983	
25 Aug 1982–01 Dec 1987	
06 Oct 1981–Nov 1981	
18 Aug 1981–18 Aug 1981	
Aug 1981–Sep 1981	
01 Jan 1981–01 Feb 1992	
Dec 1980–1981	
May 1980–Jun 1980	
25 Apr 1980	
26 Oct 1979–28 Jun 1980	
Mar 1979–15 Apr 1989	
06 Dec 1978–06 Jan 1979	
May 1978–Jun 1978	
Feb 1978–23 Mar 1978	
1978–1978	
18 Aug 1976–21 Aug 1976	
15 May 1975	
Apr 1975	
29 Apr 1975–30 Apr 1975	
11 Apr 1975–13 Apr 1975	

COLD WAR ERA

Name	Locale
Nickel Grass	Mideast
Garden Plot	USA Domestic
Red Hat	Johnston Island
Ivory Coast/Kingpin	Son Tay, Vietnam
Graphic Hand	US Domestic
Red Fox [Pueblo incident]	Korea theater
Six Day War	Mideast
CHASE	various
Powerpack	Dominican Republic
Red Dragon	Congo
[NONE]	Chinese nuclear facilities
Cuban Missile Crisis	Cuba, Worldwide
Vietnam War	Vietnam
Operation Ranch Hand	Vietnam
Operation Rolling Thunder	Vietnam
Operation Arc Light	Southeast Asia
Operation Freedom Train	North Vietnam
Operation Pocket Money	North Vietnam
Operation Linebacker I	North Vietnam
Operation Linebacker II	North Vietnam
Operation Endsweep	North Vietnam
Operation Ivory Coast/Kingpin	North Vietnam
Operation Tailwind	Laos

Dates	U.S. Forces Involved
06 Oct 1973–17 Nov 1973	
30 Apr 1972–04 May 1972	
Jan 1971–Sep 1971	
20 Nov 1970–21 Nov 1970	
1970–1970	
23 Jan 1968–05 Feb 1969	
13 May 1967–10 Jun 1967	
1967–1970	
28 Apr 1965–21 Sep 1966	
23 Nov 1964–27 Nov 1964	
15 Oct 1963–Oct 1964	
24 Oct 1962–01 Jun 1963	
15 Mar 1962–28 Jan 1973	
Jan 1962–1971	
24 Feb 1965–Oct 1968	
18 Jun 1965–Apr 1970	
06 Apr 1972–10 May 1972	
09 May 1972–23 Oct 1972	
10 May 1972–23 Oct 1972	
18 Dec 1972–29 Dec 1972	
27 Jan 1972–27 Jul 1973	
21 Nov 1970–21 Nov 1970	
1970–1970	

COLD WAR ERA

Name	Locale
Berlin	Berlin
Laos	Laos
Congo	Congo
Taiwan Straits	Taiwan Straits
Taiwan Straits	Quemoy and Matsu Islands
Blue Bat	Lebanon
Suez Crisis	Egypt
Taiwan Straits	Taiwan Straits
Korean War	Korea
Berlin Airlift	Berlin

In these several hundred wars against Communism, terrorism, drugs, or sometimes nothing much, between Pearl Harbor and Tuesday, September 11, 2001, we tended to strike the first blow. But then we're the good guys, right? Right.

Dates	U.S. Forces Involved
14 Aug 1961–01 Jun 1963	
19 Apr 1961–07 Oct 1962	
14 Jul 1960–01 Sep 1962	
23 Aug 1958–01 Jan 1959	
23 Aug 1958–01 Jun 1963	
15 Jul 1958–20 Oct 1958	
26 Jul 1956–15 Nov 1956	
11 Aug 1954–01 May 1955	
27 Jun 1950–27 July 1953	
26 Jun 1948–30 Sep 1949	

How I Became Interested in Timothy McVeigh and Vice Versa

Shredding the Bill of Rights

The Meaning of Timothy McVeigh

How I Became Interested
in Timothy McVeigh
and Vice Versa

O nce we meditate upon the unremitting violence of the United States against the rest of the world, while relying upon pretexts that, for sheer flimsiness, might have even given Hitler pause when justifying some of his most baroque lies, one begins to understand why Osama struck at us from abroad in the name of 1 billion Muslims whom we have encouraged, through our own preemptive acts of war as well as relentless demonization of them through media, to regard us in—how shall I put it?—less than an amiable light.

In the five years previous to Dark Tuesday, I had got to know the McVeigh case pretty well: in the five decades previous to that, as an enlisted soldier in World War II, as well as a narrator of our imperial history, I think I've always had an up-close view of the death struggle between the American republic, whose defender I am, and the American Global Empire, our old republic's enemy.

Osama, provoked, struck at us from afar. McVeigh, provoked, struck at us from within on April 19, 1995. Each was enraged by our government's reckless assaults upon other societies as we pursued what a great American historian has called "perpetual war for perpetual peace."

I must admit that, at first, I was not very interested in the bombing of the Murrah Federal Building in Oklahoma City because the media had so quickly and thoroughly attributed this crime to that stock American villain, the lone crazed killer, and acts of madmen are only interesting to the morbidly inclined. Also, wise Henry James had always warned writers against the use of a mad person as central to a narrative on the ground that as he was not morally responsible, there was no true tale to tell.

It was Oklahoma City that first caught my interest. It was such an unlikely place for such an astounding thing to happen. In 1907, my grandfather, Thomas Pryor Gore, brought the state into the Union; he was also elected its first senator and served until 1937. I spent my first ten years in his house in Rock Creek Park, Washington, D.C., reading to him (he was blind from childhood). I was brought up surrounded by the founders of a state that was sometimes known as the belt buckle on the Bible Belt: ironically, my grandfather was an atheist, a well-kept secret back home. Also, at the time of the First World War, Oklahoma was a base, simultaneously, for the Ku Klux Klan and for the Socialist Party, plainly an eclectic gathering place. When the Murrah Building was destroyed I misread the name as Murray, after Alfalfa Bill Murray, the state's first governor who wrote a history of the world without, it was said, ever leaving the state—or cracking a book.

In a desultory way, I began to follow the trial of McVeigh. The font of received wisdom, the *New York Times*, true to its own great tradition, found him guilty from the start. Perhaps they were, for once, I foolishly thought, acting in good faith. But as the story unfolded, it got more and more incredible. Finally, we were invited to believe that a single slight youth, with possible help from a John Doe never found by the FBI and an elusive, equally slight coconspirator, concocted a fairly complex bomb, single-handedly loaded several thousand pounds of it onto a Ryder truck, drove it to the Murrah Federal Building without blowing himself up (Northern Ireland is littered with the remains of IRA bombers who frequented rough roads with similar bombs), and then detonated it next to a many-windowed building on a bright morning, unseen. This all defied reason.

Once found guilty, however, McVeigh said that he had

done it all alone to avenge the government's slaughter of a religious cult at Waco, Texas. In a short statement to the court before sentence was passed, he quoted Supreme Court Justice Brandeis's magnificent dissent in *Olmstead*. This caught my attention. Brandeis was warning government that it was the teacher of the nation and when government broke laws it set an example that could lead only to imitation and anarchy.

Meanwhile, concerned by the airy way that various departments of our government were tidily clearing away the Bill of Rights, corner by corner, as it were, I wrote the following report for the *Vanity Fair* issue of November 1998, which McVeigh, by then on Death Row in Colorado, read and then wrote me a letter. Thus began our correspondence, which culminated in his invitation for me to witness, as his guest, his execution by lethal injection. I said I would.

Here is the piece he read in prison.

SHREDDING THE BILL OF RIGHTS

Most Americans of a certain age can recall exactly where they were and what they were doing on October 20, 1964, when word came that Herbert Hoover was dead. The heart and mind of a nation stopped. But how many recall when and how they first became aware that one or another of the Bill of Rights had expired? For me, it was sometime in 1960 at a party in Beverly Hills that I got the bad news from the constitutionally cheery actor Cary Grant. He had just flown in from New York. He had, he said, picked up his ticket at an airline counter in that magical old-world airport, Idlewild, whose very name reflected our condition. "There were these lovely girls behind the counter, and they were delighted to help me, or so they said. I signed some autographs. Then I asked one of them for my tickets. Suddenly she was very solemn. 'Do you have any identification?' she asked." (Worldly friends tell me that the "premise" of this story is now the basis of a series of TV commercials for Visa, unseen by me.) I would be exaggerating if I felt the chill in the air that long-ago Beverly Hills evening. Actually, we simply laughed. But I did, for just an instant, wonder if the future had tapped a dainty foot on our mass grave.

Curiously enough, it was Grant again who bore, as lightly as ever, the news that privacy itself hangs by a gossamer thread. "A friend in London rang me this morning," he said. This was June 4, 1963. "Usually we have code names, but this time he forgot. So after he asked for me I said into the receiver, 'All right. St. Louis, off the line. You, too, Milwaukee,' and so on. The operators love listening in. Anyway, after we talked business, he said, 'So what's the latest Hollywood gossip?' And I said, 'Well, Lana Turner is still having an affair with that black baseball pitcher.' One of the operators on the line gave a terrible cry, 'Oh, no!' "

Where Grant's name assured him an admiring audience of telephone operators, the rest of us were usually ignored. That was then. Today, in the all-out, never-to-be-won twin wars on Drugs and Terrorism, 2 million telephone conversations a year are intercepted by law-enforcement officials. As for that famous "workplace" to which so many Americans are assigned by necessity, "the daily abuse of civil liberties . . . is a national disgrace," according to the American Civil Liberties Union in a 1996 report.

Among the report's findings, between 1990 and 1996, the number of workers under electronic surveillance increased from 8 million per year to more than 30 million. Simultaneously, employers eavesdrop on an estimated 400 million telephone conversations a year—something like 750 a minute. In 1990, major companies subjected 38 percent of their employees to urine tests for drugs. By 1996, more than

70 percent were thus interfered with. Recourse to law has not been encouraging. In fact, the California Supreme Court has upheld the right of public employers to drug-test not only those employees who have been entrusted with flying jet aircraft or protecting our borders from Panamanian imperialism but also those who simply mop the floors. The court also ruled that governments can screen applicants for drugs and alcohol. This was inspired by the actions of the city-state of Glendale, California, which wanted to test all employees due for promotion. Suit was brought against Glendale on the ground that it was violating the Fourth Amendment's protection against "unreasonable searches and seizures." Glendale's policy was upheld by the California Supreme Court, but Justice Stanley Mosk wrote a dissent: "Drug testing represents a significant additional invasion of those applicants' basic rights to privacy and dignity . . . and the city has not carried its considerable burden of showing that such an invasion is justified in the case of all applicants offered employment."

In the last year or so I have had two Cary Grant–like revelations, considerably grimmer than what went on in the good old days of relative freedom from the state. A well-known acting couple and their two small children came to see me one summer. Photos were taken of their four-year-old and six-year-old cavorting bare in the sea. When the couple got home to Manhattan, the father dropped the negatives off at a drugstore to be printed. Later, a frantic call from his fortunately friendly druggist: "If I print these I've got to report you and you could get five years in the slammer for kiddie porn." The war on kiddie porn is now getting into high gear, though I was once assured by Wardell Pomeroy, Alfred Kinsey's colleague in sex research, that pedophilia was barely a blip on the statistical screen, somewhere down there with farm lads and their animal friends.

It has always been a mark of American freedom that unlike countries under constant Napoleonic surveillance, we are not obliged to carry identification to show to curious officials and pushy police. But now, due to Terrorism, every one of us is stopped at airports and obliged to show an ID that must include a mug shot[*] (something, as Allah knows, no terrorist would ever dare fake). In Chicago after an interview with Studs Terkel, I complained that since I don't have a driver's license, I must carry a passport in my own country as if I were a citizen of the old Soviet Union. Terkel has had the same trouble. "I was asked for my ID—with photo—at this southern airport, and I said I didn't have anything except the local newspaper with a big picture of

[*] As for today!

me on the front page, which I showed them, but they said that that was not an ID. Finally, they got tired of me and let me on the plane."

Lately, I have been going through statistics about terrorism (usually direct responses to crimes our government has committed against foreigners—although, recently, federal crimes against our own people are increasing). Until Dark Tuesday, only twice in twelve years has an American commercial plane been destroyed in flight by terrorists; neither originated in the United States.

The state of the art of citizen-harassment is still in its infancy. Nevertheless, new devices, at ever greater expense, are coming onto the market—and, soon, to an airport near you—including the dream machine of every horny schoolboy. The "Body Search" Contraband Detection System, created by American Science and Engineering, can "X-ray" through clothing to reveal the naked body, whose enlarged image can then be cast onto a screen for prurient analysis. The proud manufacturer boasts that the picture is so clear that even navels, unless packed with cocaine and taped over, can be seen winking at the voyeurs. The system also has what is called, according to an ACLU report, "a joystick-driven Zoom Option" that allows the operator to enlarge interesting portions of the image. During all this, the victim remains, as AS&E proudly notes, fully clothed. Orders for this machine should be addressed to the Reverend Pat Robertson and will be filled on a first-come, first-served basis, while the proud new owner of "Body Search" will be automatically included in the FBI's database of Sexual Degenerates—Class B. Meanwhile, in February 1997, the "Al" Gore Commission called for the acquisition of fifty-four high-tech bomb-detection machines known as the CTX 5000, a baggage scanner that is a bargain at $1 million and will cost only $100,000 a year to service. Unfortunately, the CTX 5000 scans baggage at the rate of 250 per hour, which would mean perhaps a thousand are needed to "protect" passengers at major airports.

Drugs. If they did not exist our governors would have invented them in order to prohibit them and so make much of the population vulnerable to arrest, imprisonment, seizure of property, and so on. In 1970, I wrote in the *New York Times*, of all uncongenial places,

> It is possible to stop most drug addiction in the United States within a very short time. Simply make all drugs available and sell them at cost. Label each drug with a precise description of what effect—good or bad—the drug will have on

the taker. This will require heroic honesty. Don't say that marijuana is addictive or dangerous when it is neither, as millions of people know— unlike "speed," which kills most unpleasantly, or heroin, which can be addictive and difficult to kick. Along with exhortation and warning, it might be good for our citizens to recall (or learn for the first time) that the United States was the creation of men who believed that each person has the right to do what he wants with his own life as long as he does not interfere with his neighbors' pursuit of happiness (that his neighbor's idea of happiness is persecuting others does confuse matters a bit).

I suspect that what I wrote twenty-eight years ago is every bit as unacceptable now as it was then, with the added problem of irritable ladies who object to my sexism in putting the case solely in masculine terms, as did the sexist founders.

I also noted the failure of the prohibition of alcohol from 1919 to 1933. And the crime wave that Prohibition set in motion so like the one today since "both the Bureau of Narcotics and the Mafia want strong laws against the sale and use of drugs because if drugs are sold at cost there would be no money in them for anyone." Will anything sensible be done? I wondered. "The American people are as devoted to the idea of sin and its punishment as they are to making money—and fighting drugs is nearly as big a business as pushing them. Since the combination of sin and money is irresistible (particularly to the professional politician), the situation will only grow worse." I suppose, if nothing else, I was a pretty good prophet.

The media constantly deplore the drug culture and, variously, blame foreign countries like Colombia for obeying that iron law of supply and demand to which we have, as a notion and as a nation, sworn eternal allegiance. We also revel in military metaphors. Czars lead our armies into wars against drug dealers and drug takers. So great is this permanent emergency that we can no longer afford such frills as habeas corpus and due process of law. In 1989 the former drug czar and TV talk-show fool, William Bennett, suggested de jure as well as de facto abolition of habeas corpus in "drug" cases as well as (I am not inventing this) public beheadings of drug dealers. A year later, Ayatollah Bennett declared, "I find no merit in the [drug] legalizers' case. The simple fact is that drug use is wrong. And the moral argument, in the end, is the most compelling argument." Of course, what this dangerous comedian thinks is moral James Madison and the Virginia statesman and Rights-man George

Mason would have thought dangerous nonsense, particularly when his "morality" abolishes their gift to all of us, the Bill of Rights. But Bennett is not alone in his madness. A special assistant to the president on drug abuse declared, in 1984, "You cannot let one drug come in and say, 'Well, this drug is all right.' We've drawn the line. There's no such thing as a soft drug." There goes Tylenol-3, containing codeine. Who would have thought that age-old palliatives could, so easily, replace the only national religion that the United States has ever truly had, anti-Communism?

On June 10, 1998, a few brave heretical voices were raised in the *New York Times*, on an inner page. Under the heading BIG NAMES SIGN LETTER CRITICIZING WAR ON DRUGS. A billionaire named "George Soros has amassed signatures of hundreds of prominent people around the world on a letter asserting that the global war on drugs is causing more harm than drug abuse itself." Apparently, the Lindesmith Center in New York, funded by Soros, had taken out an ad in the *Times*, thereby, expensively, catching an editor's eye. The signatories included a former secretary of state and a couple of ex-senators, but though the ad was intended to coincide with a United Nations special session on Satanic Substances, it carried no weight with one General Barry McCaffrey, President Clinton's war director, who called the letter "a 1950s perception," whatever that may mean. After all, drug use in the fifties was less than it is now after four decades of relentless warfare. Curiously, the *New York Times* story made the signatories seem to be few and eccentric while the Manchester *Guardian* in England reported that among the "international signatories are the former prime minister of the Netherlands . . . the former presidents of Bolivia and Colombia . . . three [U.S.] federal judges . . . senior clerics, former drugs squad officers . . ." But the *Times* always knows what's fit to print.

It is ironic—to use the limpest adjective—that a government as spontaneously tyrannous and callous as ours should, over the years, have come to care so much about our health as it endlessly tests and retests commercial drugs available in other lands while arresting those who take "hard" drugs on the parental ground that they are bad for the user's health. One is touched by their concern—touched and dubious. After all, these same compassionate guardians of our well-being have sternly, year in and year out, refused to allow us to have what every other First World country simply takes for granted, a national health service.

When Mr. and Mrs. Clinton came up to Washington, green as grass from the Arkansas hills and all pink and aglow from swift-running whitewater creeks, they tried to give the

American people such a health system, a small token in exchange for all that tax money that had gone for "defense" against an enemy that had wickedly folded when our back was turned. At the first suggestion that it was time for us to join the civilized world, there began a vast conspiracy to stop any form of national health care. It was hardly just the "right wing," as Mrs. Clinton suggested. Rather, the insurance and pharmaceutical companies combined with elements of the American Medical Association to destroy forever any notion that we be a country that provides anything for its citizens in the way of health care.

One of the problems of a society as tightly controlled as ours is that we get so little information about what those of our fellow citizens whom we will never know or see are actually thinking and feeling. This seems a paradox when most politics today involves minute-by-minute poll taking on what looks to be every conceivable subject, but, as politicians and pollsters know, it's how the question is asked that determines the response. Also, there are vast areas, like rural America, that are an unmapped ultima Thule to those who own the corporations that own the media that spend billions of dollars to take polls in order to elect their lawyers to high office.

Ruby Ridge. Waco. Oklahoma City. Three warning bells from a heartland that most of us who are urban dwellers know little or nothing about. Cause of rural dwellers' rage? In 1996 there were 1,471 mergers of American corporations in the interest of "consolidation." This was the largest number of mergers in American history, and the peak of a trend that had been growing in the world of agriculture since the late 1970s. One thing shared by the victims at Ruby Ridge and Waco, and Timothy McVeigh, who may have committed mass murder in their name in Oklahoma City, was the conviction that the government of the United States is their implacable enemy and that they can only save themselves by hiding out in the wilderness, or by joining a commune centered on a messianic figure, or, as revenge for the cold-blooded federal murder of two members of the Weaver family at Ruby Ridge, blow up the building that contained the bureau responsible for the murders.

To give the media their due, they have been uncommonly generous with us on the subject of the religious and political beliefs of rural dissidents. There is a neo-Nazi "Aryan Nations." There are Christian fundamentalists called "Christian Identity," also known as "British Israelism." All of this biblically inspired nonsense has taken deepest root in those dispossessed of their farmland in the last generation. Needless to say, Christian demagogues fan the flames of race and sectarian hatred on television and, illegally, pour church money into political campaigns.

Conspiracy theories now blossom in the wilderness like nightblooming dementia praecox, and those in thrall to them are mocked invariably . . . by the actual conspirators. Joel Dyer, in *Harvest of Rage: Why Oklahoma City Is Only the Beginning*, has discovered some very real conspiracies out there, but the conspirators are old hands at deflecting attention from themselves. Into drugs? Well, didn't you know Queen Elizabeth II is overall director of the world drug trade (if only poor Lillibet had had the foresight in these republican times!). They tell us that the Trilateral Commission is a world-Communist conspiracy headed by the Rockefellers. Actually, the commission is excellent shorthand to show how the Rockefellers draw together politicians and academics-on-the-make to serve their business interests in government and out. Whoever it was who got somebody like Lyndon LaRouche to say that this Rockefeller Cosa Nostra is really a Communist front was truly inspired.

But Dyer has unearthed a genuine ongoing conspiracy that affects everyone in the United States. Currently, a handful of agro-conglomerates are working to drive America's remaining small farmers off their land by systematically paying them less for their produce than it costs to grow, thus forcing them to get loans from the conglomerates' banks, assume mortgages, and undergo foreclosures and the sale of land to corporate-controlled agribusiness. But is this really a conspiracy or just the Darwinian workings of an efficient marketplace? There is, for once, a smoking gun in the form of a blueprint describing how best to rid the nation of small farmers. Dyer writes: "In 1962, the Committee for Economic Development comprised approximately seventy-five of the nation's most powerful corporate executives. They represented not only the food industry but also oil and gas, insurance, investment and retail industries. Almost all groups that stood to gain from consolidation were represented on that committee. Their report [*An Adaptive Program for Agriculture*] outlined a plan to eliminate farmers and farms. It was detailed and well thought out." Simultaneously, "as early as 1964, congressmen were being told by industry giants like Pillsbury, Swift, General Foods, and Campbell Soup that the biggest problem in agriculture was too many farmers." Good psychologists, the CEOs had noted that farm children, if sent to college, seldom return to the family farm. Or as one famous economist said to a famous senator who was complaining about jet lag on a night flight from New York to London, "Well, it sure beats farming." The committee got the government to send farm children to college. Predictably, most did not come back. Government then offered to help farmers relocate in other lines of work, allowing their land to be consolidated in ever vaster combines owned by fewer and fewer corporations.

So a conspiracy had been set in motion to replace the Jeffersonian ideal of a nation whose backbone was the independent farm family with a series of agribusiness monopolies where, Dyer writes, "only five to eight multinational companies have, for all intents and purposes, been the sole purchasers and transporters not only of the American grain supply but that of the entire world." By 1982 "these companies controlled 96 percent of U.S. wheat exports, 95 percent of U.S. corn exports," and so on through the busy aisles of chic Gristedes, homely Ralph's, sympathetic Piggly Wigglys.

Has consolidation been good for the customers? By and large, no. Monopolies allow for no bargains, nor do they have to fuss too much about quality because we have no alternative to what they offer. Needless to say, they are hostile to labor unions and indifferent to working conditions for the once independent farmers, now ill-paid employees. For those of us who grew up in the prewar United States there was the genuine ham sandwich. Since consolidation, ham has been so rubberized that it tastes of nothing at all while its texture is like rosy plastic. Why? In the great hogariums a hog remains in one place, on its feet, for life. Since it does not root about—or even move—it builds up no natural resistance to disease. This means a great deal of drugs are pumped into the prisoner's body until its death and transfiguration as inedible ham.

By and large, the Sherman antitrust laws are long since gone. Today three companies control 80 percent of the total beef-packing market. How does this happen? Why do dispossessed farmers have no congressional representatives to turn to? Why do consumers get stuck with mysterious pricings of products that in themselves are inferior to those of an earlier time? Dyer's answer is simple but compelling. Through their lobbyists, the corporate executives who drew up the "adaptive program" for agriculture now own or rent or simply intimidate Congresses and presidents while the courts are presided over by their former lobbyists, an endless supply of white-collar servants since two-thirds of all the lawyers on our small planet are Americans. Finally, the people at large are not represented in government while corporations are, lavishly.

What is to be done? Only one thing will work, in Dyer's view: electoral finance reform. But those who benefit from the present system will never legislate themselves out of power. So towns and villages continue to decay between the Canadian and the Mexican borders, and the dispossessed rural population despairs or rages. Hence, the apocalyptic tone of a number of recent nonreligious works of journalism and analysis that currently record, with fascinated horror, the alienation of group after group within the United States.

Since the *Encyclopaedia Britannica* is Britannica and not America, it is not surprising that its entry for "Bill of Rights, United States" is a mere column in length, the same as its neighbor on the page "Bill of Sale," obviously a more poignant document to the island compilers. Even so, they do tell us that the roots of our Rights are in Magna Carta and that the genesis of the Bill of Rights that was added as ten amendments to our Constitution in 1791 was largely the handiwork of James Madison, who, in turn, echoed Virginia's 1776 Declaration of Rights. At first, these ten amendments were applicable to American citizens only as citizens of the entire United States and not as Virginians or as New Yorkers, where state laws could take precedence according to "states' rights," as acknowledged in the tenth and last of the original amendments. It was not until 1868 that the Fourteenth Amendment forbade the states to make laws counter to the original bill. Thus every United States person, in his home state, was guaranteed freedom of "speech and press, and the right to assembly and to petition as well as freedom from a national religion." Apparently, it was Charlton Heston who brought the Second Amendment, along with handguns and child-friendly Uzis, down from Mount DeMille. Originally, the right for citizen militias to bear arms was meant to discourage a standing federal or state army and all the mischief that an armed state might cause people who wanted to live not under the shadow of a gun but peaceably on their own atop some sylvan Ruby Ridge.

Currently, the Fourth Amendment is in the process of disintegration, out of "military necessity"—the constitutional language used by Lincoln to wage civil war, suspend habeas corpus, shut down newspapers, and free southern slaves. The Fourth Amendment guarantees "the right of the people to be secure in their persons, houses, papers, and effects, against unreasonable searches and seizures . . . and no Warrants shall issue, but upon probable cause, supported by Oath or affirmation, and particularly describing the place to be searched, and the persons or things to be seized." The Fourth is the people's principal defense against totalitarian government; it is a defense that is now daily breached both by deed and law.

In James Bovard's 1994 book, *Lost Rights*, the author has assembled a great deal of material on just what our law enforcers are up to in the never-to-be-won wars against Drugs and Terrorism, as they do daily battle with the American people in their homes and cars, on buses and planes, indeed, wherever they can get at them, by hook or by crook or by sting. Military necessity is a bit too highbrow a concept for today's federal and local officials to justify their midnight smashing in of doors, usually without warning or warrant, in order to terrorize the unlucky residents.* These unlawful attacks and seizures are often justified by the possible existence of a flush toilet on the fingered premises. (If the warriors against drugs don't take drug fiends absolutely by surprise, the fiends will flush away the evidence.) This is intolerable for those eager to keep us sin-free and obedient. So in the great sign of Sir Thomas Crapper's homely invention, they suspend the Fourth, and conquer.

Nineteen ninety-two. Bridgeport, Connecticut. *The Hartford Courant* reported that the local Tactical Narcotics Team routinely devastated homes and businesses they "searched." Plainclothes policemen burst in on a Jamaican grocer and restaurant owner with the cheery cry "Stick up, niggers. Don't move." Shelves were swept clear. Merchandise ruined. "They never identified themselves as police," the *Courant* noted. Although they found nothing but a registered gun, the owner was arrested and charged with "interfering with an arrest" and so booked. A judge later dismissed the case. Bovard reports, "In 1991, in Garland, Texas, police dressed in

---

* Happily, for them, the "long war" has been declared by our Enron-Pentagon president and we are under metastasizing martial law.

black and wearing black ski-masks burst into a trailer, waved guns in the air and kicked down the bedroom door where Kenneth Baulch had been sleeping next to his seventeen-month-old son. A policeman claimed that Baulch posed a deadly threat because he held an ashtray in his left hand, which explained why he shot Baulch in the back and killed him. (A police internal investigation found no wrongdoing by the officer.) In March 1992, a police SWAT team killed Robin Pratt, an Everett, Washington, mother, in a no-knock raid carrying out an arrest warrant for her husband. (Her husband was later released after the allegations upon which the arrest warrant were based turned out to be false.)" Incidentally, this KGB tactic—hold someone for a crime, but let him off if he then names someone else for a bigger crime—often leads to false, even random allegations that ought not to be acted upon so murderously without a bit of homework first. *The Seattle Times* describes Robin Pratt's last moments. She was with her six-year-old daughter and five-year-old niece when the police broke in. As the bravest storm trooper, named Aston, approached her, gun drawn, the other police shouted, "'Get down,' and she started to crouch onto her knees. She looked up at Aston and said, 'Please don't hurt my children. . . .' Aston had his gun pointed at her and fired, shooting her in the neck. According to [the Pratt family attorney John] Muenster, she was alive another one to two minutes but could not speak because her throat had been destroyed by the bullet. She was handcuffed, lying face down." Doubtless Aston was fearful of a divine resurrection; and vengeance. It is no secret that American police rarely observe the laws of the land when out wilding with each other, and as any candid criminal judge will tell you, perjury is often their native tongue in court.

The IRS has been under some scrutiny lately for violations not only of the Fourth but of the Fifth Amendment. The Fifth requires a grand-jury indictment in prosecutions for major crimes. It also provides that no person shall be compelled to testify against himself, forbids the taking of life, liberty, or property without due process of law, or the taking of private property for public use without compensation.

Over the years, however, the ever secretive IRS has been seizing property right and left without so much as a postcard to the nearest grand jury, while due process of law is not even a concept in their single-minded pursuit of loot. Bovard notes:

> Since 1980, the number of levies—IRS seizures of bank accounts and pay checks—has increased fourfold, reaching 3,253,000 in 1992. The General Accounting Office (GAO) estimated in 1990

that the IRS imposes over 50,000 incorrect or
unjustified levies on citizens and businesses per
year. The GAO estimated that almost 6 percent
of IRS levies on business were incorrect. . . . The
IRS also imposes almost one and a half million
liens each year, an increase of over 200 percent
since 1980. *Money* magazine conducted a survey
in 1990 of 156 taxpayers who had IRS liens
imposed on their property and found that 35
percent of the taxpayers had never received a
thirty-day warning notice from the IRS of an
intent to impose a lien and that some first
learned of the liens when the magazine con-
tacted them.

The current Supreme Court has shown little interest in
curbing so powerful and clandestine a federal agency as it
routinely disobeys the Fourth, Fifth, and Fourteenth
Amendments. Of course, this particular court is essentially
authoritarian and revels in the state's exercise of power
while its livelier members show great wit when it comes to
consulting Ouija boards in order to discern exactly what
the founders originally had in mind, ignoring just how
clearly Mason, Madison, and company spelled out such

absolutes as you can't grab someone's property without first going to a grand jury and finding him guilty of a crime as law requires. In these matters, sacred original intent is so clear that the Court prefers to look elsewhere for its amusement. Lonely voices in Congress are sometimes heard on the subject. In 1993, Senator David Pryor thought it would be nice if the IRS were to notify credit agencies once proof was established that the agency had *wrongfully* attached a lien on a taxpayer's property, destroying his future credit. The IRS got whiny. Such an onerous requirement would be too much work for its exhausted employees.

Since the U.S. statutes that deal with tax regulations comprise some nine-thousand pages, even tax experts tend to foul up, and it is possible for any Inspector Javert at the IRS to find flawed just about any conclusion as to what Family X owes. But, in the end, it is not so much a rogue bureau that is at fault as it is the system of taxation as imposed by key members of Congress in order to exempt their friends and financial donors from taxation. Certainly, the IRS itself has legitimate cause for complaint against its nominal masters in Congress. The IRS's director of taxpayer services, Robert LeBaube, spoke out in 1989: "Since 1976 there have been 138 public laws modifying the Internal Revenue Code. Since the Tax Reform Act of 1986 there have been thirteen public laws changing the code, and in

1988 alone there were seven public laws affecting the code." As Bovard notes but does not explain, "Tax law is simply the latest creative interpretation by government officials of the mire of tax legislation Congress has enacted. IRS officials can take five, seven, or more years to write the regulations to implement a new tax law—yet Congress routinely changes the law before new regulations are promulgated. Almost all tax law is provisional—either waiting to be revised according to the last tax bill passed, or already proposed for change in the next tax bill."

What is this great busyness and confusion all about? Well, corporations send their lawyers to Congress to make special laws that will exempt their corporate profits from unseemly taxation: this is done by ever more complex—even impenetrable—tax laws that must always be provisional as there is always bound to be a new corporation requiring a special exemption in the form of a private bill tacked onto the Arbor Day Tribute. Senators who save corporations millions in tax money will not need to spend too much time on the telephone begging for contributions when it is time for him—or, yes, her—to run again. Unless—the impossible dream—the cost of elections is reduced by 90 percent, with no election lasting longer than eight weeks. Until national TV is provided free for national candidates and local TV for local candidates (the way civilized countries do it), there will never be tax reform. Meanwhile, the moles at the IRS, quite aware of the great untouchable corruption of their congressional masters, pursue helpless citizens and so demoralize the state.

It is nicely apt that the word *terrorist* (according to the *OED*) should have been coined during the French Revolution to describe "an adherent or supporter of the Jacobins, who advocated and practiced methods of partisan repression and bloodshed in the propagation of the principles of democracy and equality." Although our rulers have revived the word to describe violent enemies of the United States, most of today's actual terrorists can be found within our own governments, federal, state, municipal. The Bureau of Alcohol, Tobacco, and Firearms (known as ATF), the Drug Enforcement Agency, FBI, IRS, etc., are so many Jacobins at war against the lives, freedom, and property of our citizens. The FBI slaughter of the innocents at Waco was a model Jacobin enterprise. A mildly crazed religious leader called David Koresh had started a commune with several hundred followers—men, women, and children. Koresh preached world's end. Variously, ATF and FBI found him an ideal enemy to persecute. He was accused of numerous unsubstantiated crimes, including this decade's favorite, pedophilia, and was never given the benefit of due process to determine his guilt or innocence. David Kopel and Paul H. Blackman have now written the best and most detailed account of the American government's current war on its unhappy citizenry in *No More Wacos: What's Wrong with Federal Law Enforcement and How to Fix It.*

They describe, first, the harassment of Koresh and his religious group, the Branch Davidians, minding the Lord's business in their commune; second, the demonizing of him in the media; third, the February 28, 1993, attack on the commune: seventy-six agents stormed the communal buildings that contained 127 men, women, and children. Four ATF agents and six Branch Davidians died. Koresh had been accused of possessing illegal firearms even though he had previously invited law-enforcement agents into the commune to look at his weapons and their registrations. Under the Freedom of Information Act, Kopel and Blackman have now discovered that, from the beginning of what would become a siege and then a "dynamic entry" (military parlance for all-out firepower and slaughter), ATF had gone secretly to the U.S. Army for advanced training in terrorist attacks even though the Posse Comitatus Law of 1878 forbids the use of federal troops for civilian law enforcement. Like so many of our laws, in the interest of the war on Drugs, this law can be suspended if the army is requested by the Drug Law Enforcement Agency to fight sin. Koresh was secretly accused by ATF of producing methamphetamine that he was importing from nearby Mexico, three hundred miles to the south. Mayday! The army must help out. They did, though the charges against drug-hating Koresh were untrue. The destruction of the Branch Davidians had now ceased to be a civil affair where the Constitution supposedly rules. Rather, it became a matter of grave military necessity: hence a CS-gas attack (a gas that the United States had just signed a treaty swearing never to use in war) on April 19, 1993, followed by tanks smashing holes in the buildings where twenty-seven children were at risk; and then a splendid fire that destroyed the commune and, in the process, the as yet uncharged, untried David Koresh. Attorney General Janet Reno took credit and "blame," comparing herself and the president to a pair of World War II generals who could not exercise constant oversight . . . the sort of statement World War II veterans recognize as covering your ass.

Anyway, Ms. Reno presided over the largest massacre of Americans by American Feds since 1890 and the fireworks at Wounded Knee. Eighty-two Branch Davidians died at Waco, including thirty women and twenty-five children. Will our Jacobins ever be defeated as the French ones were? Ah . . . The deliberate erasure of elements of the Bill of Rights (in law as opposed to in fact when the police choose to go on the rampage, breaking laws and heads) can be found in loony decisions by lower courts that the Supreme Court prefers not to conform with the Bill of Rights. It is well known that the Drug Enforcement Agency and the IRS are inveterate thieves of private property without due process of law or redress or reimbursement later for the person who has been robbed by the state but committed no crime. Currently, according to Kopel and Blackman , U.S. and some state laws go like this: whenever a police officer is permitted, with or without judicial approval, to investigate a potential crime, the officer may seize and keep as much property associated with the alleged criminal as the police officer considers appropriate. Although forfeiture is predicated on the property's being used in a crime, there shall be no requirement that the owner be convicted of a crime. It shall be irrelevant that the person was acquitted of the crime on which the seizure was based, or was never charged with any offense. Plainly, Judge Kafka was presiding in 1987 (*United States* v. *Sandini*) when this deranged formula for theft by police was made law: "The innocence of the owner is irrelevant," declared the court. "It is enough that the property was involved in a violation to which forfeiture attaches." Does this mean that someone who has committed no crime, but may yet someday, will be unable to get his property back because *U.S.* v. *Sandini* also states firmly, "The burden of proof rests on the party alleging ownership"?

This sort of situation is particularly exciting for the woof-woof brigade of police since, according to onetime attorney general Richard Thornburgh, over 90 percent of all American paper currency contains drug residue; this means that anyone carrying, let us say, $1,000 dollars in cash will be found with "drug money," which must be seized and taken away to be analyzed and, somehow, never returned to its owner if the clever policeman knows his *Sandini*.

All across the country high-school athletes are singled out for drug testing while random searches are carried out in the classroom. On March 8, 1991, according to Bovard, at the Sandburg High School in Chicago, two teachers (their gender is not given so mental pornographers can fill in their own details) spotted a sixteen-year-old boy wearing sweatpants. Their four eyes glitteringly alert, they cased his crotch, which they thought "appeared to be 'too well endowed.'" He was taken to a locker room and stripped bare. No drugs were found, only a nonstandard scrotal sac. He was let go as there is as yet no law penalizing a teenager for being better hung than his teachers. The lad and his family sued. The judge was unsympathetic. The teachers, he ruled, "did all they could to ensure that the plaintiff's privacy was not eroded." Judge Kafka never sleeps.

Although drugs are "immoral" and must be kept from the young, thousands of schools pressure parents to give the drug Ritalin to any lively child who may, sensibly, show signs of boredom in his classroom. Ritalin renders the child docile if not comatose. Side effects? "Stunted growth, facial tics, agitation and aggression, insomnia, appetite loss, headaches, stomach pains and seizures." Marijuana would be far less harmful.

The bombing of the Alfred P. Murrah Federal Building in Oklahoma City was not unlike Dark Tuesday, a great shock to an entire nation and, one hopes, a sort of wake-up call to the American people that all is not well with us. As usual, the media responded in the only way they know how. Overnight, one Timothy McVeigh became the personification of evil. Of motiveless malice. There was the usual speculation about confederates. Grassy knollsters. But only one other maniac was named, Terry Nichols; he was found guilty of "conspiring" with McVeigh, but he was not in on the slaughter itself.

A journalist, Richard A. Serrano, has just published *One of Ours: Timothy McVeigh and the Oklahoma City Bombing*. Like everyone else, I fear, I was sick of the subject. Nothing could justify the murder of those 168 men, women, and children, none of whom had, as far as we know, anything at all to do with the federal slaughter at Waco, the ostensible reason for

McVeigh's fury. So why write such a book? Serrano hardly finds McVeigh sympathetic, but he does manage to make him credible in an ominously fascinating book.

Born in 1968, McVeigh came from a rural family that had been, more or less, dispossessed a generation earlier. Father Bill had been in the U.S. Army. Mother worked. They lived in a western New York blue-collar town called Pendleton. Bill grows vegetables; works at a local GM plant; belongs to the Roman Catholic Church. Of the area, he says, "When I grew up, it was all farms. When Tim grew up, is was half and half."

Tim turns out to be an uncommonly intelligent and curious boy. He does well in high school. He is, as his defense attorney points out, "a political animal." He reads history, the Constitution. He also has a lifelong passion for guns: motivation for joining the army. In Bush's Gulf War he was much decorated as an infantryman, a born soldier. But the war itself was an eye-opener, as wars tend to be for those who must fight them. Later, he wrote a journalist how "we were falsely hyped up." The ritual media demonizing of Saddam, Arabs, Iraqis had been so exaggerated that when McVeigh got to Iraq he was startled to "find out they are normal like me and you. They hype you to take these people out. They told us we were to defend Kuwait where the people had been raped and slaughtered. War woke me up."

As usual, there were stern laws against American troops fraternizing with the enemy. McVeigh writes a friend, "We've got these starving kids and sometimes adults coming up to us begging for food. . . . It's really 'trying' emotionally. It's like the puppy dog at the table; but much worse. The sooner we leave here the better. I can see how the guys in Vietnam were getting killed by children." Serrano notes, "At the close of the war, a very popular war, McVeigh had learned that he did not like the taste of killing innocent people. He spat into the sand at the thought of being forced to hurt others who did not hate him any more than he them."

The army and McVeigh parted once the war was done. He took odd jobs. He got interested in the far right's paranoid theories and in what Joel Dyer calls "The Religion of Conspiracy." An army buddy, Terry Nichols, acted as his guide. Together they obtained a book called *Privacy*, on how to vanish from the government's view, go underground, make weapons. Others had done the same, including the Weaver family, who had moved to remote Ruby Ridge in Idaho. Randy Weaver was a cranky white separatist with Christian

Identity beliefs. He wanted to live with his family apart from the rest of America. This was a challenge to the FBI. When Weaver did not show up in court to settle a minor firearms charge, they staked him out August 21, 1992. When the Weaver dog barked, they shot him; when the Weavers' fourteen-year-old son fired in their direction, they shot him in the back and killed him. When Mrs. Weaver, holding a baby, came to the door, FBI sniper Lon Horiuchi shot her head off. The next year the Feds took out the Branch Davidians.

For Timothy McVeigh, the ATF became the symbol of oppression and murder. Since he was now suffering from an exaggerated sense of justice, not a common American trait, he went to war pretty much on his own and ended up slaughtering more innocents than the Feds had at Waco. Did he know what he was doing when he blew up the Alfred P. Murrah Federal Building in Oklahoma City because it contained the hated bureau? McVeigh remained silent throughout his trial. Finally, as he was about to be sentenced, the court asked him if he would like to speak. He did. He rose and said, "I wish to use the words of Justice Brandeis dissenting in *Olmstead* to speak for me. He wrote, 'Our government is the potent, the omnipresent teacher. For good or ill, it teaches the whole people by its example.' " Then McVeigh was sentenced to death by the government.

Those present were deeply confused by McVeigh's quotation. How could the Devil quote so saintly a justice? I suspect that he did it in the same spirit that Iago answered Othello when asked why he had done what he had done: "Demand me nothing: what you know, you know: from this time forth I will never speak word." Now we know, too: or as my grandfather used to say back in Oklahoma, "Every pancake has two sides."

Vanity Fair
November 1998

THE MEANING OF TIMOTHY MCVEIGH

Toward the end of the last century but one, Richard Wagner made a visit to the southern Italian town of Ravello, where he was shown the gardens of the thousand-year-old Villa Rufolo. "Maestro," asked the head gardener, "do not these fantastic gardens 'neath yonder azure sky that blends in such perfect harmony with yonder azure sea closely resemble those fabled gardens of Klingsor where you have set so much of your latest interminable opera, *Parsifal?* Is not this vision of loveliness your inspiration for Klingsor?" Wagner muttered something in German. "He say," said a nearby translator, "'How about that?'"

How about that indeed, I thought, as I made my way toward a corner of those fabled gardens, where ABC-TV's *Good Morning America* and CBS's *Early Show* had set up their cameras so that I could appear "live" to viewers back home in God's country.

This was last May. In a week's time "the Oklahoma City Bomber," a decorated hero of the Gulf War, one of Nature's Eagle Scouts, Timothy McVeigh, was due to be executed by lethal injection in Terre Haute, Indiana, for being, as he himself insisted, the sole maker and detonator of a bomb that blew up a federal building in which died 168 men, women, and children. This was the greatest massacre of Americans by

an American since two years earlier, when the federal government decided to take out the compound of a Seventh-Day
Adventist cult near Waco, Texas. The Branch Davidians, as
the cultists called themselves, were a peaceful group of men,
women, and children living and praying together in antici-
pation of the end of the world, which started to come their
way on February 28, 1993. The Federal Bureau of Alcohol,
Tobacco and Firearms, exercising its mandate to "regulate"
firearms, refused all invitations from cult leader David Koresh
to inspect his licensed firearms. The ATF instead opted for
fun. More than one hundred ATF agents, without proper warrants, attacked the church's compound while, overhead, at
least one ATF helicopter fired at the roof of the main building.
Six Branch Davidians were killed that day. Four ATF agents
were shot dead, by friendly fire, it was thought.

There was a standoff. Followed by a fifty-one-day siege in
which loud music was played twenty-four hours a day outside the compound. Then electricity was turned off. Food
was denied the children. Meanwhile, the media were
briefed regularly on the evils of David Koresh. Apparently,
he was making and selling crystal meth; he was also—what
else in these sick times?—not a Man of God but a Pedophile.
The new attorney general, Janet Reno, then got tough. On
April 19 she ordered the FBI to finish up what the ATF had
begun. In defiance of the Posse Comitatus Act (a basic

bulwark of our fragile liberties that forbids the use of the
military against civilians), tanks of the Texas National
Guard and the army's Joint Task Force Six attacked the compound with a gas deadly to children and not too healthy for
adults while ramming holes in the building. Some Davidians escaped. Others were shot by FBI snipers. In an investigation six years later, the FBI denied ever shooting off
anything much more than a pyrotechnic tear-gas cannister.
Finally, during a six hour assault, the building was set fire to
and then bulldozed by Bradley armored vehicles. God saw
to it that no FBI man was hurt while more than eighty cult
members were killed, of whom twenty-seven were children.
It was a great victory for Uncle Sam, as intended by the FBI,
whose code name for the assault was Show Time.

It wasn't until May 14, 1995, that Janet Reno, on *60 Minutes*, confessed to second thoughts. "I saw what happened,
and knowing what happened, I would not do it again."
Plainly, a learning experience for the Florida daughter of a
champion lady alligator rassler.

The April 19, 1993, show at Waco proved to be the largest
massacre of Americans by their own government since 1890,
when a number of Native Americans were slaughtered at
Wounded Knee, South Dakota. Thus the ante keeps upping.

Although McVeigh was soon to indicate that he had
acted in retaliation for what had happened at Waco (he had

even picked the second anniversary of the slaughter, April 19, for his act of retribution), our government's secret police, together with its allies in the media, put, as it were, a heavy fist upon the scales. There was to be only one story: one man of incredible innate evil wanted to destroy innocent lives for no reason other than a spontaneous joy in evildoing. From the beginning, it was ordained that McVeigh was to have no coherent motive for what he had done other than a Shakespearean motiveless malignity. Iago is now back in town, with a bomb, not a handkerchief. More to the point, he and the prosecution agreed that he had no serious accomplices.

I sat on an uncomfortable chair, facing a camera. Generators hummed amid the delphiniums. *Good Morning America* was first. I had been told that Diane Sawyer would be questioning me from New York, but ABC has a McVeigh "expert," one Charles Gibson, and he would do the honors. Our interview would be something like four minutes. Yes, I was to be interviewed In Depth. This means that only every other question starts with "Now, tell us, briefly . . ." Dutifully, I told, briefly, how it was that McVeigh, whom I had never met, happened to invite me to be one of the five chosen witnesses to his execution.

Briefly, it all began in the November 1998 issue of *Vanity Fair*. I had written a piece about "the shredding of our Big of

Rights." I cited examples of IRS seizures of property without due process of law, warrantless raids and murders committed against innocent people by various drug-enforcement groups, government collusion with agribusiness's successful attempts to drive small farmers out of business, and so on. Then, as a coda, I discussed the illegal but unpunished murders at Ruby Ridge, Idaho (by the FBI) then, the next year, Waco.

When McVeigh, on appeal in a Colorado prison, read what I had written he wrote me a letter and . . .

But I've left you behind in the Ravello garden of Klingsor, where, live on television, I mentioned the unmentionable word *why*, followed by the atomic trigger word *Waco*. Charles Gibson, thirty-five hundred miles away, began to hyperventilate. "Now, wait a minute . . ." he interrupted. But I talked through him. Suddenly I heard him say, "We're having trouble with the audio." Then he pulled the plug that linked ABC and me. The soundman beside me shook his head. "Audio was working perfectly. He just cut you off." So, in addition to the governmental shredding of Amendments 4, 5, 6, 8, and 14, Mr. Gibson switched off the journalists' sacred First.

Why? Like so many of his interchangeable TV colleagues, he is in place to tell the viewers that former senator John

Danforth had just concluded a fourteen-month investigation of the FBI that cleared the bureau of any wrongdoing at
Waco. Danforth did admit that "it was like pulling teeth to
get all this paper from the FBI"

In March 1993, McVeigh drove from Arizona to Waco,
Texas, in order to observe firsthand the federal siege. Along
with other protesters, he was duly photographed by the FBI.
During the siege the cultists were entertained with twenty-
four-hour ear-shattering tapes (Nancy Sinatra: "These boots
are made for walkin' / And that's just what they'll do, / One
of these days these boots are gonna walk all over you") as
well as the recorded shrieks of dying rabbits, reminiscent of
the first George Bush's undeclared war on Panama, which
after several similar concerts outside the Vatican embassy
yielded up the master drug criminal (and former CIA.agent)
Noriega, who had taken refuge there. Like the TV networks,
once our government has a hit it will be repeated over and
over again. Oswald? Conspiracy? Studio laughter.

TV-watchers have no doubt noted so often that they are
no longer aware of how often the interchangeable TV hosts
handle anyone who tries to explain why something happened. "Are you suggesting that there was a conspiracy?" A
twinkle starts in a pair of bright contact lenses. No matter
what the answer, there is a wriggling of the body, followed
by a tiny snort and a significant glance into the camera to

show that the guest has just been delivered to the studio by flying saucer. This is one way for the public never to understand what actual conspirators—whether in the FBI or on the Supreme Court or toiling for Big Tobacco—are up to. It is also a sure way of keeping information from the public. The function, alas, of Corporate Media.

In fact, at one point, former senator Danforth threatened the recalcitrant FBI director Louis Freeh with a search warrant. It is a pity that he did not get one. He might, in the process, have discovered a bit more about Freeh's membership in Opus Dei (meaning "God's work"), a secretive international Roman Catholic order dedicated to getting its membership into high political, corporate, and religious offices (and perhaps even Heaven, too) in various lands to various ends. Lately, reluctant Medialight was cast on the order when it was discovered that Robert Hanssen, an FBI agent, had been a Russian spy for twenty-two years but also that he and his director, Louis Freeh, in the words of their fellow traveler William Rusher (*The Washington Times*, March 15, 2001), "not only [were] both members of the same Roman Catholic Church in suburban Virginia but . . . also belonged to the local chapter of Opus Dei." Mr. Rusher, once of the devil-may-care *National Review*, found this "piquant." Opus Dei was founded in 1928 by Jose-Maria Escrivá. Its lay godfather, in early years, was the Spanish dictator Francisco Franco. One of its latest paladins was the corrupt Peruvian president Alberto Fujimoro, still in absentia. Although Opus Dei tends to Fascism, the current pope has beatified Escrivá, disregarding the caveat of the Spanish theologian Juan Martin Velasco: "We cannot portray as a model of Christian living someone who has served the power of the state [the Fascist Franco] and who used that power to launch his Opus, which he ran with obscure criteria—like a Mafia shrouded in white—not accepting papal magisterium when it failed to coincide with his way of thinking."

Once, when the mysterious Mr. Freeh was asked whether or not he was a member of Opus Dei, he declined to respond, obliging an FBI special agent to reply in his stead. Special Agent John E. Collingwood said, "While I cannot answer your specific questions, I note that you have been 'informed' incorrectly."

It is most disturbing that in the secular United States, a nation whose Constitution is based upon the perpetual separation of church and state, an absolutist religious order not only has placed one of its members at the head of our secret (and largely unaccountable) police but also can now count on the good offices of at least two members of the Supreme Court.

• • •

From *Newsweek*, March 9, 2001:

> [Justice Antonin] Scalia is regarded as the embod-
> iment of the Catholic conservatives. . . . While he
> is not a member of Opus Dei, his wife Maureen
> has attended Opus Dei's spiritual functions . . .
> [while their son], Father Paul Scalia, helped con-
> vert Clarence Thomas to Catholicism four years
> ago. Last month, Thomas gave a fiery speech at
> the American Enterprise Institute, a conservative
> think-tank, to an audience full of Bush Adminis-
> tration officials. In the speech Thomas praised
> Pope John Paul II for taking unpopular stands.

And to think that Thomas Jefferson and John Adams
opposed the presence of the relatively benign Jesuit order
in our land of laws if not of God. President Bush has said
that Scalia and Thomas are the models for the sort of jus-
tices that he would like to appoint in his term of office.
Lately, in atonement for his wooing during the election of
the fundamentalist Protestants at Bob Jones University,
Bush has been "reaching out" to the Roman Catholic far
right. He is already solid with fundamentalist Protestants.
In fact, his attorney general, J. D. Ashcroft, is a Pentecostal
Christian who starts each day at eight with a prayer

meeting attended by Justice Department employees eager to be drenched in the blood of the lamb. In 1999, Ashcroft told Bob Jones University graduates that America was founded on religious principles (news to Jefferson et al.) and "we have no king but Jesus."

I have already noted a number of conspiracies that are beginning to register as McVeigh's highly manipulated story moves toward that ghastly word *closure*, which, in this case, will simply mark a new beginning. The Opus Dei conspiracy is—was?—central to the Justice Department. Then the FBI conspired to withhold documents from the McVeigh defense as well as from the department's alleged master: We the People in Congress Assembled as embodied by former senator Danforth. Finally, the ongoing spontaneous media conspiracy to demonize McVeigh, who acted alone, despite contrary evidence.

But let's return to the FBI conspiracy to cover up its crimes at Waco. Senator Danforth is an honorable man, but then, so was Chief Justice Earl Warren, and the findings of his eponymous commission on the events at Dallas did not, it is said, ever entirely convince even him. On June 1, Danforth told *The Washington Post*, "I bet that Timothy McVeigh, at some point in time, I don't know when, will be executed and after the execution there will be some box found, somewhere." You are not, Senator, just beating your gums. Also, on June 1, *The New York Times* ran an AP story in which lawyers for the Branch Davidians claim that when the FBI agents fired upon the cultists they used a type of short assault rifle that was later not tested. Our friend FBI spokesman John Collingwood said that a check of the bureau's records showed that "the shorter-barreled rifle was among the weapons tested." Danforth's response was pretty much, Well, if you say so. He did note, again, that he had got "something less than total cooperation" from the FBI. As H. L. Mencken put it, "[The Department of Justice] has been engaged in sharp practices since the earliest days and remains a fecund source of oppression and corruption today. It is hard to recall an administration in which it was not the center of grave scandal."

Freeh himself seems addicted to dull sharp practices. In 1996 he was the relentless Javert who came down so hard on an Atlanta security guard, Richard Jewell, over the Olympic Games bombing. Jewell was innocent. Even as Freeh sent out for a new hair shirt (Opus Dei members mortify the flesh) and gave the order to build a new guillotine, the FBI lab was found to have routinely bungled investigations (read *Tainting Evidence*, by J. F. Kelly and P. K. Wearne). Later, Freeh led the battle to prove Wen Ho Lee a Communist spy. Freeh's deranged charges against the blameless Los

Alamos scientist were thrown out of court by an enraged federal judge who felt that the FBI had "embarrassed the whole nation." Well, it's always risky, God's work.

Even so, the more one learns about the FBI, the more one realizes that it is a very dangerous place indeed. Kelly and Wearne, in their investigation of its lab work, literally a life-and-death matter for those under investigation, quote two English forensic experts on the subject of the Oklahoma City bombing. Professor Brian Caddy, after a study of the lab's findings: "If these reports are the ones to be presented to the courts as evidence then I am appalled by their structure and information content. The structure of the reports seems designed to confuse the reader rather than help him." Dr. John Lloyd noted, "The reports are purely conclusory in nature. It is impossible to determine from them the chain of custody, on precisely what work has been done on each item." Plainly, the time has come to replace this vast inept and largely unaccountable secret police with a more modest and more efficient bureau to be called "the United States Bureau of Investigation."

It is now June 11, a hot, hazy morning here in Ravello. We've just watched Son of Show Time in Terre Haute, Indiana. CNN duly reported that I had not been able to be a witness, as McVeigh had requested: the attorney general had given me too short a time to get from here to there. I felt somewhat better when I was told that, lying on the gurney in the execution chamber, he would not have been able to see any of us through the tinted glass windows all around him. But then members of the press who were present said that he had deliberately made "eye contact" with his witnesses and with them. He did see his witnesses, according to Cate McCauley, who was one. "You could tell he was gone after the first shot," she said. She had worked on his legal case for a year as one of his defense investigators.

I asked about his last hours. He had been searching for a movie on television and all he could find was *Fargo*, for which he was in no mood. Certainly he died in character; that is, in control. The first shot, of sodium pentothal, knocks you out. But he kept his eyes open. The second shot, of pancuronium bromide, collapsed his lungs. Always the survivalist, he seemed to ration his remaining breaths. When, after four minutes, he was officially dead, his eyes were still open, staring into the ceiling camera that was recording him "live" for his Oklahoma City audience.

McVeigh made no final statement, but he had copied out, it appeared from memory, "Invictus," a poem by W. E. Henley (1849–1903). Among Henley's numerous writings was a popular anthology called *Lyra Heroics* (1892), about those who had done selfless heroic deeds. I doubt if McVeigh ever came across it, but he would, no doubt, have identified with a group of young writers, among them Kipling, who were known as "Henley's young men," forever standing on burning decks, each a master of his fate, captain of his soul.

Characteristically, no talking head mentioned Henley's name, because no one knew who he was. Many thought this famous poem was McVeigh's work. One irritable woman described Henley as "a 19th-century cripple." I fiercely e-mailed her network: the one-legged Henley was "extremities challenged."

The stoic serenity of McVeigh's last days certainty qualified him as a Henley-style hero. He did not complain about his fate; took responsibility for what he was thought to have done; did not beg for mercy as our always sadistic media require. Meanwhile, conflicting details about him accumulate—a bewildering mosaic, in fact—and he seems more and more to have stumbled into the wrong American era. Plainly, he needed a self-consuming cause to define him. The abolition of slavery or the preservation of the Union would have been more worthy of his life than anger at the excesses of our corrupt secret police. But he was stuck where he was and so he declared war on a government that he felt had declared war on its own people.

One poetic moment in what was largely an orchestrated

hymn of hatred. Outside the prison, a group of anti-death-penalty people prayed together in the dawn's early light. Suddenly, a bird appeared and settled on the left forearm of a woman, who continued her prayers. When, at last, she rose to her feet the bird remained on her arm—consolation? *Ora pro nobis.*

CNN gave us bits and pieces of McVeigh's last morning. Asked why he had not at least said that he was sorry for the murder of innocents, he said that he could say it but he would not have meant it. He was a soldier in a war not of his making. This was Henleyesque. One biographer described him as honest to a fault. McVeigh had also noted that Harry Truman had never said that he was sorry about dropping two atomic bombs on an already defeated Japan, killing around 200,000 people, mostly collateral women and children. Media howled that that was wartime. But McVeigh considered himself, rightly or wrongly, at war, too. Incidentally, the inexorable beatification of Harry Truman is now an important aspect of our evolving imperial system. It is widely believed that the bombs were dropped to save American lives. This is not true. The bombs were dropped to frighten our new enemy, Stalin. To a man, our leading World War II commanders, including Eisenhower, C. W. Nimitz, and even Curtis LeMay (played so well by George C. Scott in *Dr. Strangelove*), were opposed to Truman's use of the bombs against a defeated enemy trying to surrender. A friend from live television, the late Robert Alan Aurthur, made a documentary about Truman. I asked him what he thought of him. "He just gives you all these canned answers. The only time I got a rise out of him was when I suggested that he tell us about his decision to drop the atomic bombs in the actual ruins of Hiroshima. Truman looked at me for the first time. 'O.K.,' he said, 'but I won't kiss their asses.'" Plainly another Henley hero, with far more collateral damage to his credit than McVeigh. Was it Chaplin's M. Verdoux who said that when it comes to calibrating liability for murder it is all, finally, a matter of scale?

After my adventures in the Ravello gardens (CBS's Bryant Gumbel was his usual low-key, courteous self and did not pull the cord), I headed for Terre Haute by way of Manhattan. I did several programs where I was cut off at the word *Waco*. Only CNN's Greta Van Susteren got the point. "Two wrongs," she said, sensibly, "don't make a right." I quite agreed with her. But then, since I am against the death penalty, I noted that three wrongs are hardly an improvement.

Then came the stay of execution. I went back to Ravello. The media were now gazing at me. Time and again I would hear or read that I had written McVeigh first, congratulating him, presumably, on his killings. I kept explaining, patiently, how, after he had read me in *Vanity Fair*, it was he who wrote me, starting an off-and-on three-year correspondence. As it turned out, I could not go so I was not able to see with my own eyes the bird of dawning alight upon the woman's arm.

The first letter to me was appreciative of what I had written. I wrote him back. To show what an eager commercialite I am—hardly school of Capote—I kept no copies of my letters to him until the last one in May.

The second letter from his Colorado prison is dated "28 Feb 99." "Mr. Vidal, thank you for your letter. I received your book United States last week and have since finished most of Part 2—your poetical musings." I should say that spelling and grammar are perfect throughout, while the handwriting is oddly even and slants to the left, as if one were looking at it in a mirror. "I think you'd be surprised at how much of that material I agree with. . . .

> As to your letter, I fully recognize that "the gen-
> eral rebellion against what our gov't has become
> is the most interesting (and I think important)
> story in our history this century." This is why I
> have been mostly disappointed at previous sto-
> ries attributing the OKC bombing to a simple act

of "revenge" for Waco—and why I was most pleased to read your Nov. article in Vanity Fair. In the 4 years since the bombing, your work is the first to really explore the underlying motivations for such a strike against the U.S. Government— and for that, I thank you. I believe that such in-depth reflections are vital if one truly wishes to understand the events of April 1995.

Although I have many observations that I'd like to throw at you, I must keep this letter to a practical length—so I will mention just one: if federal agents are like "so many Jacobins at war" with the citizens of this country, and if federal agencies "daily wage war" against those citizens, then should not the OKC bombing be considered a "counter-attack" rather than a self-declared war? Would it not be more akin to Hiroshima than Pearl Harbor? (I'm sure the Japanese were just as shocked and surprised at Hiroshima—in fact, was that anticipated effect not part and parcel of the overall strategy of that bombing?)

Back to your letter, I had never considered your age as an impediment [here he riots in tact!] until I received that letter—and noted that it was typed on a *manual typewriter*? Not to worry, recent medical studies tell us that Italy's taste for canola oil, olive oil and wine helps extend the average lifespan and helps prevent heart disease in Italians—so you picked the right place to retire to.

Again, thank you for dropping me a line—and as far as any concern over what or how to write someone "in my situation," I think you'd find that many of us are still just "regular Joes"—regardless of public perception—so there need be no special consideration(s) given to whatever you wish to write. Until next time, then . . .

Under this line he has put in quotes: "'Every normal man must be tempted at times to spit on his hands, hoist the black flag, and begin slitting throats.' —H. L. Mencken. Take good care."

He signed off with scribbled initials. Needless to say, this letter did not conform to any notion that I had had of him from reading the rabid U.S. press led, as always, by the *New York Times*, whose clumsy attempts at Freudian analysis (e.g., he was a broken blossom because his mother left his father in his sixteenth year—actually he seemed relieved). Later, there was a year or so when I did not hear from him. Two reporters from a Buffalo newspaper (he was born and raised near Buffalo) were at work interviewing him for their book, *American Terrorist*. I do think I wrote him that Mencken often resorted to Swiftian hyperbole and was not to be taken too literally. Could the same be said of McVeigh? There is always the interesting possibility—prepare for the grandest conspiracy of all—that he neither made nor set off the bomb outside the Murrah building: it was only later, when facing either death or life imprisonment, that he saw to it that he would be given sole credit for hoisting the black flag and slitting throats, to the rising fury of various "militias" across the land who are currently outraged that he is getting sole credit for a revolutionary act organized, some say, by many others. At the end, if this scenario is correct, he and the detested Feds were of a single mind.

As Senator Danforth foresaw, the government would execute McVeigh as soon as possible (within ten days of Danforth's statement to *The Washington Post*) in order not to have to produce so quickly that mislaid box with documents that might suggest that others were involved in the bombing. The fact that McVeigh himself was eager to commit what he called "federally assisted suicide" simply seemed a bizarre twist to a story that no matter how one tries to straighten it out never quite conforms to the Ur-plot of lone crazed killer (Oswald) killed by a second lone crazed

killer (Ruby), who would die in stir with, he claimed, a tale
to tell. Unlike Lee Harvey ("I'm the patsy") Oswald, our
Henley hero found irresistible the role of lone warrior
against a bad state. Where, in his first correspondence with
me, he admits to nothing for the obvious reason his lawyers
have him on appeal, in his last letter to me, April 20, 2001—
"T. McVeigh 12076-064 POB 33 Terre Haute, In. 47808
(USA)"—he writes, "Mr. Vidal, if you have read the recently
published 'American Terrorist,' then you've probably real-
ized that you hit the nail on the head with your article 'The
War at Home.' Enclosed is supplemental material to add to
that insight." Among the documents he sent was an ABC-
News.com chat transcript of a conversation with Timothy
McVeigh's psychiatrist. The interview with Dr. John Smith
was conducted by a moderator, March 29 of this year. Dr.
Smith had had only one session with McVeigh, six years earlier. Apparently McVeigh had released him from his medical
oath of confidentiality so that he could talk to Lou Michel
and Dan Herbeck, authors of *American Terrorist.*

Moderator: You say that Timothy McVeigh
"was not deranged" and that he has "no major
mental illness." So why, in your view, would he
commit such a terrible crime?

Dr. John Smith: Well, I don't think he committed it because he was deranged or misinterpreting reality. . . . He was overly sensitive, to the point of being a little paranoid, about the actions of the government. But he committed the act mostly out of revenge because of the Waco assault, but he also wanted to make a political statement about the role of the federal government and protest the use of force against the citizens. So to answer your original question, it was a conscious choice on his part, not because he was deranged, but because he was serious.

Dr. Smith then notes McVeigh's disappointment that the media had shied away from any dialogue "about the misuse of power by the federal government." Also, "his statement to me, 'I did not expect a revolution.' Although he did go on to tell me that he had had discussions with some of the militias who lived in the hills around Kingman, AZ, about how easy it would be, with certain guns in the hills there, to cut interstate 40 in two and in that sense interfere with transportation from between the eastern and western part of the United States—a rather grandiose discussion."

Grandiose but, I think, in character for those rebels who like to call themselves Patriots and see themselves as similar to the American colonists who separated from England. They are said to number from 2 million to 4 million, of whom some 400,000 are activists in the militias. Although McVeigh never formally joined any group, for three years he drove all around the country, networking with like-minded gun-lovers and federal-government-haters; he also learned, according to *American Terrorist*, "that the government was planning a massive raid on gun owners and members of the Patriot community in the spring of 1995." This was all the trigger that McVeigh needed for what he would do—shuffle the deck, as it were.

The Turner Diaries is a racist daydream by a former physics teacher writing under the pseudonym Andrew Macdonald. Although McVeigh has no hangups about blacks, Jews, and all the other enemies of the various "Aryan" white nations to be found in the Patriots' tanks, he shares the *Diaries'* obsession with guns and explosives and a final all-out war against the "System." Much has been made, rightly, of a description in the book of how to build a bomb like the one he used in Oklahoma City. When asked if McVeigh acknowledged copying this section from the novel, Dr. Smith said, "Well, sort of. Tim wanted it made clear that, unlike *The Turner Diaries*, he was not a racist. He made that very clear. He did not hate homosexuals. He made that very clear." As for the book as an influence, "he's not going to share credit with anyone." Asked to sum up, the good doctor said, simply, "I have always said to myself that if there had not been a Waco, there would not have been an Oklahoma City."

McVeigh also sent me a 1998 piece he had written for *Media Bypass*. He calls it "Essay on Hypocrisy."

> The administration has said that Iraq has no right to stockpile chemical or biological weapons . . . mainly because they have used them in the past. Well, if that's the standard by which these matters are decided, then the U.S. is the nation that set the precedent. The U.S. has stockpiled these same weapons (and more) for over 40 years. The U.S. claims that this was done for the deterrent purposes during its "Cold War" with the Soviet Union. Why, then, is it invalid for Iraq to claim the same reason (deterrence)—with respect to Iraq's (real) war with, and the continued threat of, its neighbor Iran? . . .
>
> Yet when discussion shifts to Iraq, any day-care center in a government building instantly becomes "a shield." Think about it. (Actually, there is a difference here. The administration has admitted to knowledge of the presence of

children in or near Iraqi government buildings,
yet they still proceed with their plans to bomb—
saying that they cannot be held responsible if
children die. There is no such proof, however,
that knowledge of the presence of children
existed in relation to the Oklahoma City
bombing.)

Thus, he denies any foreknowledge of the presence of children in the Murrah building, unlike the FBI, which knew
that there were children in the Davidian compound, and
managed to kill twenty-seven of them.

McVeigh quotes again from Justice Brandeis: "'Our government is the potent, the omnipresent teacher. For good or
ill it teaches the whole people by its example.'" He stops
there. But Brandeis goes on to write in his dissent, "Crime is
contagious. If the government becomes the law breaker, it
breeds contempt for laws; it invites every man to become a
law unto himself." Thus the straight-arrow model soldier
unleashed his terrible swift sword and the innocent died. But
then a lawless government, Brandeis writes, "invites anarchy.
To declare that in the administration of the criminal law the
end justifies the means—to declare that the government may
commit crimes in order to secure the conviction of a private
criminal—would bring terrible retribution."

One wonders if the Opus Dei plurality of the present Supreme Court's five-to-four majority has ever pondered these words so different from, let us say, one of its essential thinkers, Machiavelli, who insisted that, above all, the Prince must be feared.

Finally, McVeigh sent me three pages of longhand notes dated April 4, 2001, a few weeks before he was first scheduled to die. It is addressed to "C.J."(?), whose initials he has struck out.

> I explain herein why I bombed the Murrah Federal Building in Oklahoma City. I explain this not for publicity, nor seeking to win an argument of right or wrong. I explain so that the record is clear as to my thinking and motivations in bombing a government installation.
>
> I chose to bomb a Federal Building because such an action served more purposes than other options. Foremost, the bombing was a retaliatory strike: a counter-attack, for the cumulative raids (and subsequent violence and damage) that federal agents had participated in over the preceding years (including, but not limited to, Waco). From the formation of such units as the FBI's "Hostage Rescue" and other assault teams amongst federal

agencies during the 80s, culminating in the Waco incident, federal actions grew increasingly militaristic and violent, to the point where at Waco, our government—like the Chinese—was deploying tanks against its own citizens.

. . . For all intents and purposes, federal agents had become "soldiers" (using military training, tactics, techniques, equipment, language, dress, organization and mindset) and they were escalating their behavior. Therefore, this bombing was also meant as a pre-emptive (or pro-active) strike against those forces and their command and control centers within the federal building. When an aggressor force continually launches attacks from a particular base of operations, it is sound military strategy to take the fight to the enemy. Additionally, borrowing a page from U.S. foreign policy, I decided to send a message to a government that was becoming increasingly hostile, by bombing a government building and the government employees within that building who represent that government. Bombing the Murrah Federal Building was morally and strategically equivalent to the U.S. hitting a government building in Serbia, Iraq, or other nations. Based

on observations of the policies of my own government, I viewed this action as an acceptable
option. From this perspective what occurred in
Oklahoma City was no different than what Americans rain on the heads of others all the time, and,
subsequently, my mindset was and is one of clin-
ical detachment. (The bombing of the Murrah
Building was not personal no more than when
Air Force, Army, Navy or Marine personnel bomb
or launch cruise missiles against (foreign) government installations and their personnel.)

I hope this clarification amply addresses your
question.

Sincerely,

T.M.

USP Terre Haute (In.)

There were many outraged press notes and letters when I
said that McVeigh suffered from "an exaggerated sense of
justice." I did not really need the adjective except that I
knew that few Americans seriously believe that anyone is
capable of doing anything except out of personal self-
interest, while anyone who deliberately risks—and gives—
his life to alert his fellow citizens to an onerous

government is truly crazy. But the good Dr. Smith put that one in perspective: McVeigh was not deranged. He was serious.

It is June 16. It seems like five years rather than five days since the execution. The day before the execution, June 10, the *New York Times* discussed "The Future of American Terrorism." Apparently, terrorism has a real future; hence we must beware Nazi skinheads in the boondocks. The *Times* is, occasionally, right for the usual wrong reasons. For instance, their current wisdom is to dispel the illusion that "McVeigh is merely a pawn in an expansive conspiracy led by a group of John Does that may even have had government involvement. But only a small fringe will cling to this theory for long." Thank God: one had feared that rumors of a greater conspiracy would linger on and Old Glory herself would turn to fringe before our eyes. The *Times*, more in anger than in sorrow, feels that McVeigh blew martyrdom by first pleading not guilty and then by not using his trial to "make a political statement about Ruby Ridge and Waco." McVeigh agreed with the *Times*, and blamed his first lawyer, Stephen Jones, in unholy tandem with the judge, for selling him out. During his appeal, his new attorneys claimed that the serious sale took place when Jones, eager for publicity, met

with the *Times*'s Pam Belluck. McVeigh's guilt was quietly
conceded, thus explaining why the defense was so feeble.
(Jones claims he did nothing improper.)

Actually, in the immediate wake of the bombing, the *Times*
concedes, the militia movement skyrocketed from 220
antigovernment groups in 1995 to more than 850 by the end
of '96. A factor in this growth was the belief circulating
among militia groups "that government agents had planted
the bomb as a way to justify anti-terrorism legislation. No less
than a retired Air Force general has promoted the theory that
in addition to Mr. McVeigh's truck bomb, there were bombs
inside the building." Although the *Times* likes analogies to
Nazi Germany, they are curiously reluctant to draw one
between, let's say, the firing of the Reichstag in 1933 (Göring
later took credit for this creative crime), which then allowed
Hitler to invoke an Enabling Act that provided him with all
sorts of dictatorial powers "for protection of the people and
the state," and so on to Auschwitz.

The canny *Portland Free Press* editor, Ace Hayes, noted that
the one absolutely necessary dog in every terrorism case has
yet to bark. The point to any terrorist act is that credit must be
claimed so that fear will spread throughout the land. But no
one took credit until McVeigh did, *after* the trial, in which he
was condemned to death as a result of circumstantial evidence

produced by the prosecution. Ace Hayes wrote, "If the bombing was not terrorism then what was it? It was pseudo terrorism, perpetrated by compartmentalized covert operators for the purposes of state police power." Apropos Hayes's conclusion, Adam Parfrey wrote in *Cult Rapture*, "[The bombing] is not different from the bogus Viet Cong units that were sent out to rape and murder Vietnamese to discredit the National Liberation Front. It is not different from the bogus 'finds' of Commie weapons in El Salvador. It is not different from the bogus Symbionese Liberation Army created by the CIA/FBI to discredit the real revolutionaries." Evidence of a conspiracy? Edye Smith was interviewed by Gary Tuchman, May 23, 1995, on CNN. She duly noted that the ATF bureau, about seventeen people on the ninth floor, suffered no casualties. Indeed they seemed not to have come to work that day. Jim Keith gives details in *OKBOMB!*, while Smith observed on TV, "Did the ATF have a warning sign? I mean, did they think it might be a bad day to go into the office? They had an option not to go to work that day, and my kids didn't get that option." She lost two children in the bombing. ATF has a number of explanations. The latest: five employees were in the offices, unhurt.

Another lead not followed up: McVeigh's sister read a letter he wrote her to the grand jury stating that he had become a member of a "Special Forces Group involved in criminal activity."

• • •

At the end, McVeigh, already condemned to death, decided to take full credit for the bombing. Was he being a good professional soldier, covering up for others? Or did he, perhaps, now see himself in a historic role with his own private Harper's Ferry, and though his ashes molder in the grave, his spirit is marching on? We may know—one day.

As for "the purposes of state police power," after the bombing, Clinton signed into law orders allowing the police to commit all sorts of crimes against the Constitution in the interest of combating terrorism. On April 20, 1996 (Hitler's birthday of golden memory, at least for the producers of *The Producers*), President Clinton signed the Anti-Terrorism Act ("for the protection of the people and the state"—the emphasis, of course, is on the second noun), while, a month earlier, the mysterious Louis Freeh had informed Congress of his plans for expanded wiretapping by his secret police. Clinton described his Anti-Terrorism Act in familiar language (March 1, 1993, *USA Today*): "We can't be so fixated on our desire to preserve the rights of ordinary Americans." A year later (April 19, 1994, on MTV): "A lot of people say there's too much personal freedom. When personal freedom's being abused, you have to move to limit it." On that plangent note he graduated cum laude from the Newt Gingrich Academy.

In essence, Clinton's Anti-Terrorism Act would set up a national police force, over the long-dead bodies of the founders. Details are supplied by H.R. 97, a chimera born of Clinton, Reno, and the mysterious Mr. Freeh. A twenty-five-hundred-man Rapid Deployment Strike Force would be organized, under the attorney general, with dictatorial powers. The chief of police of Windsor, Missouri, Joe Hendricks, spoke out against this supra-Constitutional police force. Under this legislation, Hendricks said, "an agent of the FBI could walk into my office and commandeer this police department. If you don't believe that, read the crime bill that Clinton signed into law.... There is talk of the Feds taking over the Washington, D.C., police department. To me this sets a dangerous precedent." But after a half-century of the Russians are coming, followed by terrorists from proliferating rogue states as well as the ongoing horrors of drug-related crime, there is little respite for a people so routinely—so fiercely—disinformed. Yet there is a native suspicion that seems to be a part of the individual American psyche—as demonstrated in polls, anyway. According to a Scripps Howard News Service poll, 40 percent of Americans think it quite likely that the FBI set the fires at Waco. Fifty-one percent believe federal officials killed Jack Kennedy (Oh, Oliver what hast thou wrought!). Eighty percent believe that the military is withholding evidence that Iraq used nerve gas or something as deadly in the Gulf. Unfortunately, the other side of this coin is troubling. After Oklahoma City, 58 percent of Americans, according to the *Los Angeles Times*, were willing to surrender some of their liberties to stop terrorism—including, one wonders, the sacred right to be misinformed by government?

Shortly after McVeigh's conviction, Director Freeh soothed the Senate Judiciary Committee: "Most of the militia organizations around the country are not, in our view, threatening or dangerous." But earlier, before the Senate Appropriations Committee, he had "confessed" that his bureau was troubled by "various individuals, as well as organizations, some having an ideology which suspects government of world-order conspiracies—individuals who have organized themselves against the United States." In sum, this bureaucrat who does God's Work regards as a threat those "individuals who espouse ideologies inconsistent with principles of Federal Government." Oddly, for a former judge, Freeh seems not to recognize how chilling this last phrase is.

The CIA's former director William Colby is also made nervous by the disaffected. In a chat with Nebraska state senator John Decamp (shortly before the Oklahoma City bombing), he mused, "I watched as the Anti-War movement rendered it impossible for this country to conduct or win the Viet Nam War. . . . This Militia and Patriot movement . . . is far more significant and far more dangerous for Americans than the Anti-War movement ever was, if it is not intelligently dealt with. . . . It is not because these people are armed that America need be concerned." Colby continues, "They are dangerous because there are so many of them. It is one thing to have a few nuts or dissidents. They can be dealt with, *justly or otherwise* [my emphasis] so that they do not pose a danger to the system. It is quite another situation when you have a true movement— millions of citizens believing something, particularly when the movement is made up of society's average, successful citizens." Presumably one "otherwise" way of handling such a movement is when it elects a president by a half-million votes—to call in a like-minded Supreme Court majority to stop a state's recounts, create arbitrary deadlines, and invent delays until our ancient electoral system, by default, must give the presidency to the "system's" candidate as opposed to the one the people voted for.

Many an "expert" and many an expert believe that McVeigh neither built nor detonated the bomb that blew up a large part of the Murrah Federal Building on April 19, 1995. To start backward—rather the way the FBI conducted this case—if McVeigh was *not* guilty, why did he confess to the murderous deed? I am convinced from his correspondence and what one has learned about him in an ever lengthening row of books that, once found guilty due to what he felt was the slovenly defense of his principal lawyer, Stephen Jones, so unlike the brilliant defense of his "co-conspirator" Terry Nichols's lawyer Michael Tigar, McVeigh believed that the only alternative to death by injection was a half-century or more of life in a box. There is another aspect of our prison system (considered one of the most barbaric in the First World) that was alluded to by a British writer in *The Guardian*. He quoted California's attorney general, Bill Lockyer, on the subject of the C.E.O. of an electric utility, currently battening on California's failing energy supply. "'I would love to personally escort this CEO to an 8 by 10 cell that he could share with a tattooed dude who says—"Hi, my name is Spike, Honey."' . . . The senior law official in the state was confirming (what we all suspected) that rape is penal policy. Go to prison and serving as a Hell's Angel sex slave is judged part of your sentence." A couple of decades fending off Spike is not a Henley hero's idea of a good time. Better dead than Spiked. Hence, "I bombed the Murrah building."

Evidence, however, is overwhelming that there was a plot involving militia types and government infiltrators—who knows?—as prime movers to create panic in order to get Clinton to sign that infamous Anti-Terrorism Act. But if, as it now appears, there were many interested parties involved, a sort of unified-field theory is never apt to be

found, but should there be one, Joel Dyer may be its Einstein. (Einstein, of course, never got his field quite together,
either.) In 1998, I read Dyer's *Harvest of Rage*. Dyer was
editor of the *Boulder Weekly*. He writes on the crisis of rural
America due to the decline of the family farm, which also
coincided with the formation of various militias and religious cults, some dangerous, some merely sad. In *Harvest of
Rage*, Dyer made the case that McVeigh and Terry Nichols
could not have acted alone in the Oklahoma City bombing.
Now he has, after long investigation, written an epilogue to
the trials of the two coconspirators.

It will be interesting to see if the FBI is sufficiently intrigued
by what Joel Dyer has written to pursue the leads that he
has so generously given them.

Thus far, David Hoffman's *The Oklahoma City Bombing
and the Politics of Terror* is the most thorough of a dozen or
two accounts of what did and did not happen on that day
in April. Hoffman begins his investigation with retired air-
force brigadier general Benton K. Partin's May 17, 1995,
letter delivered to each member of the Senate and House of
Representatives: "When I first saw the pictures of the truck-
bomb's asymmetrical damage to the Federal Building, my

immediate reaction was that the pattern of damage would have been technically impossible without supplementing demolition charges at some of the reinforcing concrete column bases. . . . For a simplistic blast truck-bomb, of the size and composition reported, to be able to reach out in the order of 60 feet and collapse a reinforced column base the size of column A-7 is beyond credulity." In separate agreement was Samuel Cohen, father of the neutron bomb and formerly of the Manhattan Project, who wrote an Oklahoma state legislator, "It would have been absolutely impossible and against the laws of nature for a truck full of fertilizer and fuel oil . . . no matter how much was used . . . to bring the building down." One would think that McVeigh's defense lawyer, restlessly looking for a Middle East connection, could certainly have called these acknowledged experts to testify, but a search of Jones's account of the case, *Others Unknown*, reveals neither name.

In the March 20, 1996, issue of *Strategic Investment* newsletter, it was reported that Pentagon analysts tended to agree with General Partin. "A classified report prepared by two independent Pentagon experts has concluded that the destruction of the Federal building in Oklahoma City last April was caused by five separate bombs. . . . Sources close to the study say Timothy McVeigh did play a role in the bombing but 'peripherally,' as a 'useful idiot.'" Finally, inevitably—this is wartime, after all—"the multiple bomb-ings have a Middle Eastern 'signature,' pointing to either Iraqi or Syrian involvement."

As it turned out, Partin's and Cohen's pro bono efforts to examine the ruins were in vain. Sixteen days after the bombing, the search for victims stopped. In another letter to Congress, Partin stated that the building should not be destroyed until an independent forensic team was brought in to investigate the damage. "It is also easy to cover up cru-cial evidence as was apparently done in Waco. . . . Why rush to destroy the evidence?" Trigger words: the Feds demol-ished the ruins six days later. They offered the same excuse that they had used at Waco, "health hazards." Partin: "It's a classic cover-up."

Partin suspected a Communist plot. Well, nobody's perfect.

"So what's the take-away?" was the question often asked by TV producers in the so-called golden age of live televi-sion plays. This meant: what is the audience supposed to think when the play is over? The McVeigh story presents us with several take-aways. If McVeigh is simply a "useful idiot," a tool of what might be a very large conspiracy, involving various homegrown militias working, some think, with Middle Eastern helpers, then the FBI's refusal to follow up so many promising leads goes quite beyond its ordinary incompetence and smacks of treason. If McVeigh was the unlikely sole mover and begetter of the bombing, then his "inhumane" (the Unabomber's adjective) destruction of so many lives will have served no purpose at all unless we take it seriously as what it is, a wake-up call to a federal government deeply hated, it would seem, by millions. (Remember that the popular Ronald Reagan always ran *against* the federal government, though often for the wrong reasons.) Final far-fetched take-away: McVeigh did not make nor deliver nor detonate the bomb but, once arrested on another charge, seized all "glory" for himself and so gave up his life. That's not a story for W. E. Henley so much as for one of his young men, Rudyard Kipling, author of *The Man Who Would Be King*.

Finally, the fact that the McVeigh-Nichols scenario makes no sense at all suggests that yet again, we are confronted with a "perfect" crime—thus far.

Vanity Fair
September 2001

FALLOUT

FALLOUT

O nce our media has invented a cartoon image for a national villain or hero, it does not take a benign view of anyone who contradicts its version. My reasonably mild analysis of McVeigh was interpreted as approval of the bombing at Oklahoma City and I was said to have hailed him as "a freedom fighter," a phrase, as you have seen, that I never used. I thought it was obvious that I agreed with the examining psychiatrist who said, "Had there been no Waco, there would have been no Oklahoma City." Therefore, the truth-seeker should concentrate on the various elements that led up to the federal massacre at Waco on the ground that whatever the Federal government does it does in the name of all of us. What McVeigh did he did on his own for reasons well worth understanding since he appears to represent, in many ways, millions of heartland Americans.

In the original article I quote Joel Dyer at greater length

than I do now. He had spent years following up on leads to potential coconspirators with McVeigh. There was even a potential Iraqi connection in Oklahoma City, which might well have brought roses to the cheeks of our right-wing activists, eager for war with Iraq as well as Iran, Somalia, and just about any Islamic nation that does not obey us. In any case, I have now left out all those leads not followed by the FBI on the ground that the spoor, as Tarzan used to say, grows, with passing time, ever more faint.

But at the time Dyer and I were ready to share our findings, no matter how unwanted, with the FBI. The mysterious Louis Freeh had left as director and his place was taken by R. S. Mueller, for whom I prepared the following letter, which I read on NBC's *Today Show*, leaving out the names of those who had given leads, but including the document numbers of the FBI reports collected by Dyer during various "discovery" court hearings.

August 27, 2001

The Honorable Robert S. Mueller III, Director-Designate
Federal Bureau of Investigation
J. Edgar Hoover Building
935 Pennsylvania Avenue, N.W.
Washington, D.C. 20535-0001

Dear Director-Designate Mueller:

Congratulations on your recent appointment as director
of the Federal Bureau of Investigation. If recent news
reports are to be believed, it seems your first priority
is to restore the tattered image of the Freeh-based
bureau. We see you as Shane come to town. With that in
mind, might I suggest a bona fide investigation of the
Oklahoma City bombing? To that worthy end, I am providing
you a list of "302" reports from the Bureau's alleged
"investigation" that I hope you will find more interesting than did your predecessor Mr. Louis Freeh.

McVeigh Discovery Materials
302 Reports

DCNO 005290001-1	DCNO 004623001-1
DCNO 016598001-1	DCNO 004622001-1
DCNO 004412001-1	Russell Roe DCNO#—illegible
DCNO 004613001-1	
DCNO 016417001-1	DCNO 007936001-1
DCNO 006333001-1	DCNO 008597001-1
DCNO 015040001-1	DCNO 015830001-1
DCNO 015042001-1	DCNO 016016001-1
DCNO 015039001-1	DCNO 007986001-1
DCNO 015041001-1	Lead # 15004 DCNO#—illegible

Upon review, you will find that these 19 "302" reports
were generated as a result of your organization's inter-
views with Kansas law enforcement personnel, eyewit-
nesses, confidential informants, militia members, etc.
Collectively, they contain information regarding, among

other things, four men, resident in East Kansas at the time of the Oklahoma City bombing, who were well-known anti-U.S. government radicals.

Let me briefly summarize the contents of these documents.

In the first series of documents is a report of perhaps the only eyewitness to the actual assemblage of the bombing components. He was present, on or about April 17, 1995, at Geary Lake and identified one man and others unknown who were offloading fertilizer from a farm truck to the Ryder truck.

The second set of reports deals with a man who was over-heard, several weeks prior to the bombing, saying that "Someone is going to smoke some Okies—wait till Timmy does his job." It is also noted that this same individual had suggested committing numerous acts of terrorism—both prior to and subsequent to—the OKC bombing. In fact, your agency later arrested him for one such plot. Let us hope they will tell you about it.

A third group of "302"s describes in detail a man said to be a dangerous, government-hating radical thought to have exploded fertilizer bombs on his remote Kansas property prior to the fertilizer-bomb explosion in Oklahoma City. You should have no trouble locating information on this individual, as your agency has had many unusual dealings with him over the years. In an effort to save you valuable time, as I am sure you are quite busy cleaning up after Mr. Freeh, please be aware that if you simply request this individual's file by the original number assigned by the F.B.I. (W924376484), you may encounter difficulty in locating it because, I've been told, this file number was mysteriously reassigned to an unrelated case in New Jersey and that new numbers have been issued for the Kansas man's files. What, one wonders, can this mean?

The last set of reports contains information from Kansas law enforcement, describing an anti-government radical living in the same small town as Terry Nichols,

McVeigh's only named co-conspirator. You will also find
his name on the Posse Comitatus videotapes seized by
the F.B.I. at the Nichols's brothers' farm in Michigan.
I believe the seized tapes describe him as a close personal friend of the Posse leader whose phone number was
in Mr. Nichols's wallet at the time of his arrest. But
then again, perhaps these two likeminded friends of a
friend never stumbled across one another in a town
whose population is 636.

In addition to the above information, these reports
also indicate that these men had ties to both the
Michigan Militia and the Arizona Patriots, two anti-
government organizations with which Mr. McVeigh associated prior to the bombing.

Here are my concerns and, I suspect, the concerns of
every thoughtful American. Based upon an examination of
the evidence turned over during the discovery process
and trial, it appears that the F.B.I., despite the
quality of the leads I've set forth above, never actually bothered to pursue the information provided in any
substantive manner. The men in question were not interviewed, not even the obligatory "Where were you on
April 19?" phone call. In fact, they were not investigated in any manner whatsoever, no vehicle registration
checks, nothing. By the way, I think you would find the
vehicle angle quite interesting. Had the above leads
been investigated in even a cursory manner, the FBI
would have learned that all four men were closely associated in the same radical anti-government faction. I'm
sure you will agree that such a connection between
these overlooked leads might tell us who did what that
cruel April day.

In addition, as set out in my recent article in *Vanity
Fair*, the name of at least one other person associated
with this same organization was given to the F.B.I. by
three different persons, yet there were no "302"
reports concerning the three and no information whatsoever on the subject in the discovery materials turned
over by the government.

I cannot say with certainty that these men were part of the bombing plot that left 168 innocent people dead. It would be impossible to reach such a bold conclusion in light of the F.B.I.'s failure to even investigate such a possibility. I am simply pointing out that the government's ongoing insistence that it "followed every lead" and that there is "no credible evidence that others were involved" is not based on the evidence, but rather on the F.B.I.'s increasingly jittery public relations department. The evidence turned over thus far in this case suggests an indifference to the very notion of justice that goes quite beyond the bureau's eerie incompetence. To be generous, I suspect that the bureau did pursue more leads than it has ever let on, so, as Senator Danforth suggested before McVeigh's execution: after the execution there will be some box found, somewhere, containing evidence that was withheld from McVeigh's defense attorneys.

Now that McVeigh has already been injected into a better world, I am sure that the bureau's choice of explanation to my inquiry will be a difficult one. Was it an incompetent investigation, as this trail of ignored leads would suggest? Or is it something even more sinister, a case of withholding evidence during discovery, which is a criminal act? Either way, I believe that the American people, particularly those most affected by the murderous bombing, deserve an explanation.

Please reply at your earliest convenience.

Sincerely,

Gore Vidal
Care of *Vanity Fair*
4 Times Square, 22nd Floor
New York, NY 10036

For those readers now hanging from what Alfalfa Bill Murray

used to call "tender-hooks," what did the Director-Designate reply? Nothing. Also, as far as anyone can tell, the Lee Harvey Oswald scenario has played out yet again. I will say that when I was questioned on NBC—why did I bring this up and so add to the unique suffering of the Oklahomans?—I said I bring it up to save them and the rest of the country from further suffering because potential enemies of the United States are still at large and they are certain to strike at us again. I was not sufficiently prescient to say that some, even as I spoke, were studying in Oklahoma on how to maneuver aircraft in the air without first taking off.

Finally, McVeigh spoke to me from the grave. I received a note from Eric F. Magnuson, director of the World Libertarian Order. On May 21, 2001, Mr. Magnuson wrote McVeigh on Death Row asking him what changes he would make in the way the United States administers itself. McVeigh duly responded with ten additions to the ten amendments that comprise our Bill of Rights. Here they are, preceded by Mr. Magnuson's position on the matter:

ERIC F. MAGNUSON'S DISCLAIMER

June 20, 2001. It must be stressed here that the WLO does not necessarily agree with any of Timothy McVeigh's ideas just because we reproduce them here. Our writings are entirely separate from his. We certainly do not advocate or condone the blowing up of large buildings filled with people that one does not even know. You might kill a future Libertarian. We do feel however, that these tragic things cannot be kept from happening in the future unless we are willing to take a very clear and honest look at why they have happened in the past. We are confident that all right-thinking people agree with this very basic principle. Those who disagree are those who prefer fantasy to truth. Such people are the problem, not any part of the solution. The fact that Timothy McVeigh did a desperate and destructive thing does not conveniently negate the fact that government in America has become too large and oppressive, it simply underscores it.

Eric F. Magnuson
Director
The World Libertarian Order

TIM'S BILL OF RIGHTS

1.) Neither Speech, Press, Religion, nor Assembly shall be infringed, nor shall such be forced upon any person by the government of the United States.

2.) There shall be no standing military force during peace-time, (this) to include large bodies of federal law enforcers or coalitions of these officers that would constitute a military force, with the exception of sea-based maritime forces.

3.) The Executive Office shall hold no power to unilaterally alter Constitutional rights.

4.) No person shall be subjected to any form of direct taxation or wage withholdings by the Federal government.

5.) No person's life or liberty shall be taken without due process. Any government employee circumventing due process rights shall be punished with imprisonment. Citizens shall not be subjected to invasions of their homes or property by employees of the Federal government. Property or other assets of United States citizens shall not be subject to forfeiture to the Federal government.

6.) Personal activities that do not infringe upon the rights or property of another shall not be charged, prosecuted, or punished by the United States government. Any crime alleged will be prosecuted by the jurisdiction most local to the alleged crime, respectively. No person shall be twice tried for an offense alleged and adjudicated in another jurisdiction. No person shall be subjected to cruel and unusual punishment, nor shall the Federal government hold power to execute any individual as punishment for a crime convicted, or contract to another entity for this purpose. No person shall be held to account for the actions of another, unless proven by more than one witness to be the principal figure.

7.) All currency shall be redeemable in a globally recognized material of intrinsic value, such as silver.

8.) Legislative members shall earn no more than twice the current poverty level and shall not be subject to any additional pay, bonuses, rewards, gifts, entitlements, or other such privileges, as holding such office is meant to serve the people and should not be looked upon as a capitalist career opportunity.

9.) Where non-violent checks and balances fail to remedy government abuse or tyranny, the common people reserve the right to rebellion. Inherent with this right, the common people maintain the absolute right to own and possess those weapons which are used by any level of government for domestic policing.

10.) Any rights not enumerated here belong inherently to the people or the state respectively, and shall not be assumed by omission (to be) delegated to the jurisdiction of the Federal government.

Timothy J. McVeigh
28 May 2001

THE NEW THEOCRATS

THE NEW THEOCRATS

June 18, 1997, proved to be yet another day that will live in infamy in the history of *The Wall Street Journal*, or t.w.m.i.p., "the world's most important publication," as it bills itself—blissfully unaware of just how unknown this cheery neofascist paper is to the majority of Americans, not to mention those many billions who dwell in darkness where the sulfurous flashes of Wall Street's little paper are no more than marsh gas from the distant marches of the loony empire. June 18 was the day that t.w.m.i.p. took an ad in the *New York Times*, the paper that prints only the news that will fit its not-dissimilar mind-set. The ad reprinted a t.w.m.i.p. editorial titled "Modern Morality," a subject I should have thought alien to the core passions of either paper. But then for Americans morality has nothing at all to do with ethics or right action or who is stealing what money—and liberties—from whom. Morality is SEX. SEX. SEX.

The edit's lead is piping hot. "In the same week that an Army general with 147 Vietnam combat missions" (remember the *Really* Good War, for lots of Dow Jones listings?) "ended his career over an adulterous affair 13 years ago" (t.w.m.i.p. is on strong ground here; neither the general nor the lady nor any other warrior should be punished for adulteries not conducted while on watch during enemy attack) "the news broke"—I love that phrase in a journal of powerful opinion and so little numberless news—"that a New Jersey girl gave birth to a baby in the bathroom at her high school prom, put it in the trash and went out to ask the deejay to play a song by Metallica—for her boyfriend. The baby is dead."

Misled by the word "girl," I visualized a panicky pubescent tot. But days later, when one Melissa Drexler was indicted for murder, she was correctly identified by the *Times* as a "woman, 18." In a recently published photograph of her alongside her paramour at the prom, the couple look to be in their early thirties. But it suited t.w.m.i.p. to misrepresent Ms. Drexler as yet another innocent child corrupted by laissez-faire American liberal "values," so unlike laissez-faire capitalism, the great good.

All this is "moral chaos," keens the writer. I should say that all this is just plain old-fashioned American stupidity where a religion-besotted majority is cynically egged on by a ruling establishment whose most rabid voice is *The Wall Street Journal.*

"We have no good advice on how the country might extricate itself anytime soon from a swamp of sexual confusion. . . ." You can say that again and, of course, you will. So, rather than give bad advice, cease and desist from taking out ads to blame something called The Liberals. In a country evenly divided between political reactionaries and religious maniacs, I see hardly a liberal like a tree—or even a burning bush—walking. But the writer does make it clear that the proscribed general was treated unfairly while the "girl" with baby is a statistic to be exploited by right-wing journalists, themselves often not too far removed from the odious Metallica-listening orders who drop babies in johns, a bad situation that might have been prevented by the use, let us say, of a rubber when "girl" and "boy" had sex.

But, no. We are assured that the moral chaos is the result of sexual education and "littering," as the ad puts it, "the swamp" with "condoms that for about the past five years have been dispensed by adults running our high schools . . . or by machines located in, by coincidence, the bathroom." Presumably, the confessional would be a better venue, if allowed. So, on the one hand, it is bad, as we all agree, for a woman to give birth and then abandon a baby; but then too, it's wrong, for some metaphysical reason, to help prevent such a birth from taking place. There is no sense of cause/effect when these geese start honking. Of course, t.w.m.i.p. has its own agendum: outside marriage, no sex of any kind for the lower classes and a policing of everyone, including generals and truly valuable people, thanks to the same liberals who now "forbid nothing and punish anything." This is spaceship-back-of-the-comet reasoning.

The sensible code observed by all the world (except for certain fundamentalist monotheistic Jews, Christians, and Muslims) is that "consensual" relations in sexual matters are no concern of the state. The United States has always been backward in these matters, partly because of its Puritan origins and partly because of the social arrangements arrived at during several millennia of family-intensive agrarian life, rudely challenged a mere century ago by the Industrial Revolution and the rise of the cities and, lately, by the postindustrial work-world of services in which "safe" prostitution should have been, by now, a bright jewel.

Although the "screed" (a favorite right-wing word) in the *Times* ad is mostly rant and not to be taken seriously, the spirit behind all this blather is interestingly hypocritical. T.w.m.i.p. is not interested in morality. In fact, any company that can increase quarterly profits through the poisoning of a river is to be treasured. But the piece does reflect a certain unease that the people at large, most visibly through sex, may be trying to free themselves from their masters, who grow ever more stern and exigent in their prohibitions—one strike and you're out is their dirty little secret. In mid-screed, the paper almost comes to the point: "Very simply [*sic*], what we're suggesting here is that the code of sexual behavior formerly set down by established religion in the U.S. more or less kept society healthy, unlike the current manifest catastrophe." There it is. Where is Norman Lear, creator of *Mary Hartman, Mary Hartman*, now that we need him? Visualize on the screen gray clapboard, slate-colored sky, om*ni*-ous (as Darryl Zanuck used to say) music. Then a woman's plaintive voice calling "Hester Prynne, Hester Prynne!" as the screen fills with a pulsing scarlet "A."

So arrière-garde that it is often avant-garde, t.w.m.i.p. is actually on to something. Although I shouldn't think anyone on its premises has heard of the eighteenth-century Neapolitan scholar Vico, our readers will recall that Vico, working from Plato, established various organic phases in human society. First, Chaos. Then Theocracy. Then Aristocracy. Then Democracy—but as republics tend to become imperial and tyrannous, they collapse and we're back to Chaos and to its child Theocracy, and a new cycle. Currently, the United States is a mildly chaotic imperial republic headed for the exit, no bad thing unless there is a serious outbreak of Chaos, in which case a new age of religion will be upon us. Anyone who ever cared for our old Republic, no matter how flawed it always was with religious exuberance, cannot *not* prefer Chaos to the harsh rule of Theocrats. Today, one sees them at their savage worst in Israel and in certain Islamic countries, like Afghanistan, etc. Fortunately, thus far their social regimentation is still no match for the universal lust for consumer goods, that brave new world at the edge of democracy. As for Americans, we can still hold the fort against our very own praying mantises—for the most part, fundamentalist Christians abetted by a fierce, decadent capitalism in thrall to totalitarianism as proclaimed so saucily in the *New York Times* of June 18, 1997.

The battle line is now being drawn. Even as the unfortunate "girl" in New Jersey was instructing the deejay, the Christian right was organizing itself to go after permissiveness in entertainment. On June 18 the Southern Baptists at their annual convention denounced the Disney company and its TV network, ABC, for showing a lesbian as a human being, reveling in *Pulp Fiction* violence, flouting Christian family values. I have not seen the entire bill of particulars (a list of more than one hundred "properties" to be boycotted was handed out), but it all sounds like a pretrial deposition from Salem's glory days. Although I have criticized the Disney cartel for its media domination, I must now side with the challenged octopus.

This is the moment for Disney to throw the full weight of its wealth at the Baptists, who need a lesson in constitutional law they will not soon forget. They should be brought to court on the usual chilling-of-First-Amendment grounds as well as for restraint of trade. Further, and now let us for once get to the root of the matter. The tax exemptions for the revenues of all the churches from the Baptists to the equally absurd—and equally mischievous—Scientologists must be removed.

The original gentlemen's agreement between Church and State was that *We the People* (the State) will in no way help or hinder any religion while, absently, observing that as religion is "a good thing," the little church on Elm Street won't have to pay a property tax. No one envisaged that the most valuable real estate at the heart of most of our old cities would be tax-exempt, as churches and temples and orgone boxes increased their holdings and portfolios. The *quo* for this huge *quid* was that religion would stay out of politics and not impose its superstitions on *Us the People*. The agreement broke down years ago. The scandalous career of the Reverend Presidential Candidate Pat Robertson is a paradigm.

As Congress will never act, this must be a grass-roots

movement to amend the Constitution, even though
nothing in the original First Amendment says a word about
tax exemptions or any other special rights to churches,
temples, orgone boxes. This is a useful war for Disney to
fight, though I realize that the only thing more cowardly
than a movie studio or TV network is a conglomerate forced
to act in the open. But if you don't, Lord Mouse, it will be
your rodentian ass 15.7 million Baptists will get, not to
mention the asses of all the rest of us.

The Nation
21 July 1997

A Letter to Be Delivered

A Letter to Be Delivered

I am writing this note a dozen days before the inauguration of the loser of the year 2000 presidential election. We are now faced with a Japanese seventeenth-century-style arrangement: a powerless Mikado ruled by a shogun vice president and his Pentagon warrior counselors. Do they dream, as did the shoguns of yore, of the conquest of China? We shall know more soon, I should think, than late. Sayonara.

11 January 2001

*Congratulations, Mr. President-Elect. Like everyone else, I'm eagerly looking forward to your inaugural address. As you must know by now, we could never get enough of your speeches during the recent election in which the best man

*This was written for *Vanity Fair* before the November 7, 2000, presidential election.

won, as he always does in what Spiro Agnew so famously called "the greatest nation in the country."

Apropos your first speech to us as president. I hope you don't mind if I make a few suggestions, much as I used to do in the sixties when I gave my regular States of the Union roundups on David Susskind's TV show of blessed memory. Right off, it strikes me that this new beginning may be a good place to admit that for the last fifty years we have been waging what the historian Charles A. Beard so neatly termed "perpetual war for perpetual peace."

It is my impression, Mr. President-Elect, that most Americans want our economy converted from war to peace. Naturally, we still want to stand tall. We also don't want any of our tax money wasted on health care because that would be Communism, which we all abhor. But we would like some of our tax dollars spent on education. Remember what you said in your terminal debate with your opponent, now so much charred and crumbling toast? "Education is the key to the new millennium." (Actually, looking at my notes, all four of you said that.)

In any case, it is time we abandon our generally unappreciated role as world policeman, currently wasting Colombia, source of satanic drugs, while keeping Cuba, Iraq, and, until recently, Serbia "in correction," as policepersons call house arrest. This compulsive interference in the affairs of other states is expensive and pointless. Better we repair our own country with "internal improvements," as Henry Clay used to say. But in order to do this your first big job will be to curb the Pentagon warlords and their fellow conspirators in Congress and the boardrooms of corporate America. Ever since the Soviet Union so unsportingly disbanded in order to pursue protocapitalism and double-entry bookkeeping, our warlords have been anxiously searching for new enemies in order to justify an ever increasing military budget. Obviously, there is Terrorism to be fought. There is also the war on Drugs, to be fought but never won. Even so, in the failed attempt, the coming destruction of Colombia, a once liberal democratic nation, promises to be great fun for warlords and media, if not the residents of a once happy nation. Lately, a new clear and present danger has been unveiled: Rogue States, or "states of concern." Currently, North Korea, Iraq, and Iran have been so fingered, while the world's 1 billion Muslims have been demonized as crazed fanatics, dedicated to destroying all that is good on earth, which is us.

Since we have literally targeted our enemies, the Pentagon assumes that, sooner or later, Rogues will take out our cities, presumably from spaceships. So to protect ourselves, the Ronald Reagan Memorial Nuclear Space Shield must be set in place at an initial cost of $60 billion even though, as of July, tests of the system, no matter how faked by the

Pentagon, continued to fail. The fact that, according to polls, a majority of your constituents believe that we already have such a shield makes it possible for you to say you're updating it and then do nothing. After all, from 1949 to 1999 the United States spent $7.1 trillion on "national defense." As a result, the national debt is $5.6 trillion, of which $3.6 trillion is owed to the public, and $2 trillion to the Social Security–Medicare Trust Funds, all due to military spending and to the servicing of the debt thus incurred.

Mr. President-Elect, since Treasury figures are traditionally juggled, it would be nice if you were to see to it that the actual income and outgo of federal money are honestly reported. Last year the government told us, falsely, that its income was just over $1.8 trillion while it spent just under $1.8 trillion; hence, the famous, phantom surplus when there was, of course, our usual homely deficit of around $90 billion. Year after year, the government's official income is inflated by counting as revenue the income of the people's Social Security and Medicare Trust Funds. These funds are not federal revenue. This year Social Security has a healthy surplus of $150 billion. No wonder corporate America and its employees in Congress are eager to privatize this healthy fund, thus far endangered only by them.

Although actual military spending was indeed lower last year than usual, half the budget still went to pay for wars

to come as well as to blowing up the odd aspirin factory in
the Sudan. Cash outlays for the military were $344 billion
while interest on the military-caused national debt was
$282 billion: sorry to bore you with these statistics, but
they are at the heart of our—what was Jimmy Carter's
unfortunate word?—malaise (that's French for broke). The
Clinton administration's cheery promise of a $1.8 trillion
budget surplus over the next decade was, of course, a bold
if comforting fiction, based on surreal estimates of future
federal income—not to mention expenditures that, if anything like last September's congressional spending spree,
will drown us in red ink.

Sir, if you are going to be of any use at all to the nation
and to the globe that it holds hostage, you will have to
tame the American military. Discipline the out-of-control
service chiefs. Last September, the chairman of the Joint
Chiefs of Staff, General H. H. Shelton, declared that more,
not less, dollars were needed. Specifically, the Marines want
an extra $1.5 billion per year, the army wants over $30 billion, the navy $20 billion, the air force $30 billion, all in
the absence of an enemy (we spend twenty-two times more
than our seven potential enemies—Cuba, Iran, Iraq, Libya,
North Korea, Sudan, and Syria—combined). You must not
grant these ruinous increases.

• • •

In August 1961, I visited President Kennedy at Hyannis Port. The Berlin Wall was going up, and he was about to begin a huge military buildup—reluctantly, or so he said, as he puffed on a cigar liberated by a friend from Castro's Cuba. It should be noted that Jack hated liberals more than he did conservatives. "No one can ever be liberal enough for the *New York Post*," he said. "Well, the *Post* should be happy now. Berlin's going to cost us at least three and a half billion dollars. So, with this military buildup, we're going to have a seven-billion-dollar deficit for the year. That's a lot of pump priming." He scowled. "God, I hate the way they throw money around over there at the Pentagon."

"It's not they," I said. "It's you. It's your administration." Briskly, he told me the facts of life, and I repeat them now as advice from the thirty-fifth to the—what are you, Mr. President? Forty-third president? "The only way for a president to control the Pentagon would be if he spent the entire four years of his first term doing nothing else but investigating that mess, which means he really could do nothing else . . ."

"Like getting reelected?"

He grinned. "Something like that."

So I now propose, Mr. President-Elect, while there is still time, that you zero in on the links between corporate America and the military and rationalize as best you can the various procurement policies, particularly the Ronald Reagan Memorial Nuclear Shield. You should also leak to the American people certain Pentagon secrets. In 1995, we still had our missiles trained on 2,500 foreign targets. Today, to celebrate peace in the world, our missiles are trained on 3,000 foreign targets—of which 2,260 are in Russia; the rest are directed at China and the Rogue States. Although President Clinton has spoken eloquently of the need for a reduction in such dangerous nuclear targeting, the Pentagon does as it pleases, making the world unsafe for everyone. But then *USA Today* recently reported that the military enjoys the highest popularity rating (64 percent) of any group in the country—the Congress and Big Business are among the lowest. Of course, the services do spend $265 million annually on advertising.

Jack Kennedy very much enjoyed Fletcher Knebel's thriller *Seven Days in May*, later a film. The story: a jingo based on the real-life Admiral Arthur Radford plans a military coup to take over the White House. Jack found the book riveting. "Only," he chuckled, rather grimly, "it's a lot more likely that this president will one day raise his own army and occupy their damned building." No, I don't agree with Oliver Stone that the generals killed him. But there is, somewhere out there, a watchdog that seems never to bark in the night. Yet the dog that doesn't bark is the one that should be guarding the house from burglars, in this case the military-industrial complex that President Eisenhower so generously warned us against. Although there are many media stories about costly overruns in the defense industries as well as the slow beginning of what may yet turn into an actual debate over the nuclear shield that Reagan envisaged for us after seeing Alfred Hitchcock's *Torn Curtain*, a movie nowhere near as good as *Seven Days in May*, there is, as yet, no debate over the role of the military in the nation's life and its ongoing threat to us all, thanks to the hubris of senior officers grown accustomed to dispensing vast amounts of the people's money for missiles that can't hit targets and bombers that can't fly in the rain. Congress, which should ride herd, does not because too many of its members are financed by those same companies that absorb our tax money, nor is it particularly helpful that senior officers, after placing orders with the defense industries, so often go to work as salesmen for the very same companies they once bought from.

Of all recent presidents, Clinton was expected to behave the most sensibly in economic matters. He understood how the economy works. But because he had used various dodges to stay out of the Vietnam War, he came to office ill at ease with the military. When Clinton tried to live up to his pledge to gay voters that the private life of any military person was no one's business but his own, the warlords howled that morale would be destroyed. Clinton backed down. When Clinton went aboard the aircraft carrier U.S.S. *Theodore Roosevelt* to take the salute, sailors pranced around with mop ends on their heads, doing fag imitations while hooting at the president, who just stood there. These successful insults to civilian authority have made the military ever more truculent and insolent. And now they must be brought to heel.

This summer, the warlords of the Pentagon presented the secretary of defense with their Program Objective Memorandum. Usually, this is a polite wish list of things that they would like to see under the Christmas tree. By September, the wish list sounded like a harsh ultimatum. As one dissenting officer put it, "Instead of a budget based on a top-line budget number, the chiefs are demanding a budget based on military strategy." Although their joint military strategies, as tested in war over the last fifty years, are usually disastrous, military strategy in this context means simply extorting from the government $30 billion a year over and above the 51 percent of the budget that now already goes for war. Mr. President-Elect, I would advise you to move your office from the West Wing of the White House to the Pentagon, across the river. Even though every day that you spend there could prove to be your Ides of March, you will at least have the satisfaction of knowing that you tried to do something for us, the hitherto unrepresented people.

Fifty years ago, Harry Truman replaced the old republic with a national-security state whose sole purpose is to wage perpetual wars, hot, cold, and tepid. Exact date of replacement? February 27, 1947. Place: White House Cabinet Room. Cast: Truman, Undersecretary of State Dean Acheson, a handful of congressional leaders. Republican senator Arthur Vandenberg told Truman that he could have his militarized economy only *if* he first "scared the hell out of the American people" that the Russians were coming. Truman obliged. The perpetual war began. Representative government of, by, and for the people is now a faded memory. Only corporate America enjoys representation by the Congresses and presidents that it pays for in an arrangement where no one is entirely accountable because those who have bought the government also own the media. Now, with the revolt of the Praetorian Guard at the Pentagon, we are entering a new and dangerous phase. Although we regularly stigmatize other societies as rogue states, we ourselves have become the largest rogue state of all. We honor no treaties. We spurn international courts. We strike unilaterally wherever we choose. We give orders to the United Nations but do not pay our dues. We complain of terrorism, yet our empire is now the greatest terrorist of all. We bomb, invade, subvert other states. Although We the People of the United States are the sole source of legitimate authority in this land, we are no longer represented in Congress Assembled. Our Congress has been hijacked by corporate America and its enforcer, the imperial military machine. We the unrepresented People of the United States are as much victims of this militarized government as the Panamanians, Iraqis, or Somalians. We have allowed our institutions to be taken over in the name of a globalized American empire that is totally alien in concept to anything our founders had in mind. I suspect that it is far too late in the day for us to restore the republic that we lost a half-century ago.

Even so, Mr. President-Elect, there is an off chance that you might actually make some difference if you start now to rein in the warlords. Reduce military spending, which will make you popular because you can then legitimately reduce our taxes instead of doing what you have been financed to do, freeing corporate America of its small tax burden. The 1950 taxes on corporate profits accounted for 25 percent of federal revenue; in 1999 only 10.1 percent. Finally, as sure as you were not elected by We the People but by the vast sums of unaccountable corporate money, the day of judgment is approaching. Use your first term to break the Pentagon. Forget about a second term. After all, if

you succeed on the other side of the Potomac, you will be
a hero to We the People. Should you fail or, worse, do
nothing, you may be the last president, by which time history will have ceased to notice the United States and all our
proud rhetoric will have been reduced to an ever dimin-
ishing echo. Also, brood upon an odd remark made by your
canny, if ill-fated, predecessor Clinton. When Gingrich and
his Contract on (rather than with) America took control of
Congress, Clinton said, "The president is not irrelevant."
This was a startling admission that he could become so.
Well, sir, be relevant. Preserve, protect, and defend what is
left of our ancient liberties, not to mention our heavily
mortgaged fortune.*

Vanity Fair
December 2000

---

*And so Mr. President, elected by the Supreme Court (5–4), has now, in addi-
tion to a vice president who was a former secretary of defense, appointed
another former defense secretary to his old post as well as a general to be secretary of state; thus the pass was sold. We are now in, the president tells us, "a
long war"—presumably to the end.